Dark Victory

Transnational Institute Series

The Transnational Institute is an independent fellowship of researchers and activists living in different parts of the world, who develop innovative analyses of world affairs.

It serves no government, political party or interest group.

Other titles in the TNI series:

For details of forthcoming titles in the TNI series, please contact Pluto Press

Dark Victory

The United States and Global Poverty

NEW EDITION

Walden Bello

with

Shea Cunningham and Bill Rau

Foreword by
Susan George

Pluto  Press

with

and
Transnational Institute (TNI)

First published 1994 by Pluto Press
345 Archway Road, London N6 5AA
in association with the
Institute for Food and Development Policy (Food First),
398 60th Street, Oakland, California 94618, USA;
and with the Transnational Institute (TNI),
Paulus Potterstraat 20, 1071 DA, Amsterdam

Second edition 1999

British Library Cataloguing in Publication Data
A catalogue record for this book is available from the British Library

ISBN 0 7453 1466 X hbk (worldwide)
ISBN 0 7453 1461 9 pbk (ex. US)

Library of Congress Cataloging-in-Publication Data
Bello, Walden F.
    Dark Victory : The United States and global poverty / Walden Bello
with Shea Cunningham and Bill Rau ; Foreword by Susan George. — 2nd
ed. / with a new epilogue by Walden Bello.
        p.   cm.
    Includes bibliographical references and index.
    ISBN 0–935028–76–5
    1. Structural adjustment (Economic policy)—Developing countries.
2. Poverty—Developing countries. 3. International Monetary Fund-
–Developing countries. 4. World Bank—Developing countries.
5. United States—Economic policy—1981–1993. 6. United States–
–Foreign economic relations—Developing countries. 7. Developing
countries—Foreign economic relations—United States. 8. Supply
-side economics—United States. 9. Economic history—1971–1990.
I. Cunningham, Shea. II. Rau, Bill. III. Title.
HC59.7.B3873 1998
337.73—dc21   98–47956
                                                              CIP

Food First paperback edition (US only)
ISBN 0 935028 76 5

Produced for the publishers by
Chase Production Services, Chadlington, OX7 3LN
Typeset from disk by
Stanford Desktop Publishing Services, Northampton
Printed in the EC by The Cromwell Press, Trowbridge

Contents

About the Author and his Associates

Walden Bello is currently professor of sociology and public administration at the University of the Philippines and co-director of Focus on the Global South, a program of research, analysis, and advocacy based at the Chulalongkorn University Social Research Institute in Bangkok, Thailand. He also served as executive director of the the Institute for Food and Development Policy (Food First) in Oakland, California from 1990–94.

Earlier, Dr Bello worked in Washington, DC as a lobbyist for democratic rights in the Philippines. He obtained his PhD in sociology from Princeton University in 1975 and has taught at the University of California.

Dr Bello is author of, among other books, *People and Power in the Pacific: the Struggle for the Post-Cold War Order* (Pluto Press, 1992), *Dragons in Distress: Asia's Miracle Economies in Crisis* (Penguin, 1991), co-authored with Stephanie Rosenfeld, *Brave New Third World? Strategies for Survival in the Global Economy* (Earthscan, 1990), *American Lake: Nuclear Peril in the Pacific* (Penguin, 1987), co-authored with Peter Hayes and Lyuba Zarsky and *A Siamese Tragedy: Development and Disintegration in Modern Thailand* (Zed, 1998), co-authored with Shea Cunningham and Li Kheng Poh.

Shea Cunningham has served as a research associate of both Food First and Focus on the Global South. **Bill Rau**, an expert on Africa, is on the Board of Directors of the Washington, DC based Africa Policy Information Center.

About Food First

The Institute for Food and Development Policy, commonly known as Food First, is a non-profit research and educational center based in Oakland, USA, and Manila, Philippines. Food First focuses on issues of hunger and democracy around the world. Founded in 1975 by Frances Moore Lappé, author of *Diet for a Small Planet*, and by Joseph Collins, the Institute has worked to change accepted views on the causes of, and solutions to, world hunger. It has also been actively promoting the vision of participatory, equitable, and ecologically sustainable development in the Third World.

Becoming a Member

Nearly all of our income comes from our members and from sales of our books. We do not accept contributions from government sources. Because the Institute is not tied to any government, it can speak with a strong independent voice, free from ideological formulas and prevailing government policies. You can support our efforts by joining Food First. For more information, and a free catalog of our publications, write or call:

The Institute for Food and Development Policy,
398 60th Street,
Oakland,
California 94618, USA
Tel: (510) 654-4400
Fax: (510) 654-4551

Acknowledgements

This work is dedicated to Dr Patrocinio Angeles and Ms Leonila San Miguel, who have long served as models of disinterested service to the community for the author.

This book started out as an exploration of current trends in global poverty and expanded into an investigation of structural adjustment in the Third World, the debt crisis, trade wars with the so-called NICs ('newly industrializing countries'), the restructuring of the American economy, and the reformulation of defense policy in the post-Cold War era.

Naturally, the author and his collaborators are indebted to the analysis, research, and policy work conducted by numerous specialists in these areas. But, in particular, we owe a debt of gratitude to Franz Schurmann, Martin Khor, Susan George, Steve Hellinger, Doug Hellinger, Yoke-Ling Chee, Vandana Shiva, Chakravarthi Raghavan, Renato Constantino, Robin Broad, John Cavanagh, Richard Falk, Alicia Korten, Charles Abugre, Joan French, David Korten, Joyce Kolko, Bruce Rich, Lyuba Zarsky, Leonor Briones, Sisuwan Kuankachoen, Chad Dobson, Patricia Adams, Sixto Roxas, Thea Lee, Randy Hayes, Sandy Close, Men Sta. Ana, Gabriel Kolko, Davidson Budhoo, Peter Hayes, Ross Hammond, Fran Korten, Joel Rocamora, Josh Karliner, Dan Smith, Mohamad Idris, Junie Kalaw, Isagani Serrano, Maria Clara Soares, Witoon Permpongsacharoen, Development GAP, Transnational Institute, Institute for Policy Studies, International Rivers Network, Freedom from Debt Coalition (Philippines), Project for Ecological Recovery (Thailand), Third World Network, Green Forum (Philippines), Bank Information Center, Rain Forest Action Network, and Economic Policy Institute.

This book would not have been possible without the assistance, advice, and encouragement provided by the following colleagues: Paula Fomby, Marilyn Borchardt, Roger Van Zwanenberg, Crosby Milne, John Gershman, Kira Nam, Stephanie Rosenfeld, Martha Katigbak, Ann Evans, Beatriz Manz, Denise Newman, Priscilla Enriquez, Marybeth Braun, Paul Haible, Soheir Morsy, Angela Siscamanis, Annette Olson, J. Gonzales, Jake Sproull, Toni Bird, and D. Kinley.

For providing seed funding for this project, we would like to thank Mike Roque and the Committee for the Self-Development of Peoples of the Presbyterian Church (USA) and Mia Adjahi and the United Methodist Church Women's Division.

The key arguments in this book were originally outlined in a short article that appeared in *Christianity and Crisis* in February 1992. CIC has now ceased publication after over 50 years of exemplary service in the cause of social justice. To its editors, particularly Leon Howell and Tom Kelly, we owe much gratitude for their support over the years.

The second half of this book was written while the author was a visiting fellow of the Institute of Asian Studies of Chulalongkorn University in Bangkok in 1993. For their warm support, we would like to thank Professor Withaya Sucharithanarugse, Suda Suntisavekul and the staff of the Institute of Asian Studies, as well as Professor Suthy Prasartset of the Department of Economics.

Finally, through personal support, camaraderie, or simply giving tips on light, fictional reading, the following friends helped see us through the project: Marilen Abesamis, Greg Young, Annette Ferrer, Ami Ferrer, Tonette Garcia, Emalyn Lapus, Kay Eisenhower, Jim Goodno, Daisy Leyva, Rebecca Ratcliffe, Brida Brennan, Nonoy Hacbang, and Oranut Supaphanwadee.

None of these colleagues and friends is, of course, to be blamed for errors of analysis and fact that this book might contain. For these we are solely responsible.

WB, SC, BR

San Francisco
July 27, 1993

Foreword

Susan George

Dark Victory sounds like a '40s film title, with brave pilots, courageous sweethearts and a happy ending – the villains punished, the heroes rewarded and everything morally neat and tidy as democracy triumphs over fascism. No such luck here. This book and for that matter the world of the '90s aren't like that. The vile and the villainous are getting their way, overcoming every obstacle, crushing all opposition in their path.

But wait! They too may get their come-uppance in the next millennium; those who appear supremely confident today are in fact running scared; they have overstretched their reach and are in inexorable decline. They have led us into a kind of late, very late, Roman Empire on a global scale and the only sure thing is that at the end of this particular movie, the set will be littered with bodies.

Walden Bello and his colleagues Shea Cunningham and Bill Rau explain here exactly what happened in the 1980s. It happened so fast you could well have missed it if you were looking the other way. Very few scholars have, up to now, attempted to show how all the pieces fit together. Reaganism and Thatcherism were only the tip of this iceberg, a world-wide phenomenon called 'rollback'.

This strategy, the child of the new conservative establishment and of transnational, mostly US, capital was to the South what the policy of containment was to the East. Rollback meant an end to Third World pretensions. There was to be no more talk of a New International Economic Order, binding codes of conduct for foreign investors, mandatory transfers of technology or managed commodity prices. The South was to return to that quiescent state from which it should never have been allowed to emerge. The unruly would be disciplined and the rebellious cowed.

Bello *et al* build their case with relentless scholarship. The familiar cycle of debt, balance of payments crises and adjustment under the tutelage of the World Bank and the International Monetary Fund is crisply laid out; its consequences as well. Even those who think they know the structural adjustment scenario inside out will be grateful to Bello for taking on the toughest cases for examination – countries like Mexico, Chile, Costa Rica or Ghana, often cited by the Bank and the Fund as star pupils. The stars are decidedly tarnished when Bello has finished with them. The debt-cum-adjustment crisis is shown for what it is – a protracted war against the poor.

Less well known is the parallel war against that more limited part of the South which is not head-over-heels in debt and is therefore immune to discipline via structural adjustment.

Competition from the Newly Industrialising Countries – the famous dragons or tigers – is unwelcome, though their increasingly opulent markets are coveted. Dragons are made to be slain and tigers to be hunted; trade regulations and penalties will do as well as lances and rifles.

The war against the South is accompanied by another war on the home front, this time against the work force inside the United States. Here is quintessential Reaganism on its own ground, bringing home the iron law of economics to the millions: the point of capitalism is not to provide decent jobs at decent wages but to make as large a profit as possible. End of story.

One could wish that Bello *et al.* had made more of the complicity of Southern élites who, on the whole, lie back and enjoy rollback because they, too, profit hugely from it. A North versus South, Empire versus Barbarian scenario, yes, but another serious player is the transnational élite to match transnational capital, sitting pretty at the top, with everyone else underneath. The world-as-sphere, North–South, is also world-as-pyramid and those at the apex are not all white.

In these ongoing wars, nearly everyone loses and the slim hope for change lies in the fact that they may decide that they will not lose quietly. A dubious battle indeed that leads to such victory – be it dark or hollow.

List of Acronyms

AFDC	Aid to Families with Dependent Children (US)
CIEC	Conference on International Economic Cooperation
GATT	General Agreement on Tariffs and Trade
GDP	Gross Domestic Product
GSP	General System of Preferences
IBM	International Business Machines
IDA	International Development Association
IDB	International Development Bank
IMF	International Monetary Fund
MFA	Multifiber Agreement
MITI	Ministry for International Trade and Industry (Japan)
NACF	National Agricultural Cooperatives' Federation (Korea)
NAFTA	North American Free Trade Agreement
NIC	Newly Industrializing Country
NIEO	New International Economic Order
OECD	Organization for Economic Co-operation and Development
OPEC	Organization of Petroleum Exporting Countries
PAMSCAD	Program of Actions to Mitigate the Social Costs of Adjustment (Ghana)
PATCO	Professional Air Controllers' Union (US)
POSCO	Pohang Iron and Steel Company (Korea)
SAF	structural adjustment facility
SAL	structural adjustment loan
SAP	structural adjustment program
SUNFED	Special United Nations Fund for Development
TRIMS	Trade Related Investment Measures
TRIPS	Trade Related Intellectual Property Rights
UN	United Nations
UNCTAD	United Nations Conference on Trade and Development
UNDP	United Nations Development Program
UNESCO	United Nations Educational, Scientific and Cultural Organization
UNICEF	United Nations Children's Fund
USTR	United States Trade Representative
VER	Voluntary Export Restraint

Introduction: The Great Reversal

This new order will not put an end to history. It will not be a utopia, harmonious and placid. Indeed, conflict is more likely now that the Cold War has ended and the market has triumphed ... For inequality will cleave the new world order as surely as the Berlin Wall once divided East and West.

—Jacques Attali, *Millenium: Winners and Losers in the Coming World Order* (New York: Times Books, 1991)

For many people in the West the defining event of the last few years has been the collapse of centralized socialism in the Soviet Union and Eastern Europe.

Springtime of Freedom ...

Socialist regimes were largely undermined by their internal short-comings, particularly their inability to institutionalize democracy and their failure to create an economy that would promote equity without stifling growth and innovation and destroying the environment. There was a rough equality in living conditions under centralized socialist rule, but it was not the dynamic equality amid rising living standards and growing freedom that had been envisioned by the pioneers of socialism. Rather, it was the equitable sharing of shoddy material goods and services amid generalized economic stagnation, political repression, and environmental collapse.

Thus, the peoples of the South for the most part wished the citizens of Eastern Europe and the former Soviet Union well as the latter began to exercise their newly found political freedoms. Many of them, however, could not understand the rush of the post-socialist leaders to embrace free-market reforms and, in some cases, economic 'shock treatments' prescribed by the World Bank and the International Monetary Fund (IMF). In their view, it was these very methods that had led to the massive reversal of the fortunes of the Third World during the 1980s.

1

... or Time of Troubles?

By the beginning of the 1990s, per capita income in Africa had plunged to the level it had held at the time of political independence in the 1960s. In Latin America, per capita income was down to where it had been in the late 1970s.[1] Indeed, for the peoples of the South, the defining features of the last two decades of the twentieth century have been the rollback of their living standards, the virtual loss of their economic sovereignty, and the increased hollowness of their political independence – all of which add up to what Chakravarthi Raghavan has so aptly called 'recolonization'.[2]

The eagerness for reforms designed to release the energies of private enterprise on the part of Eastern European technocrats failed to excite not only people in the Third World but large sectors of the population in the United States and Western Europe as well. Many Americans viewed pro-market reforms as in fact measures to promote the unrestrained freedom of corporate capitalism, and they bitterly attacked these policies as the cause of the sharp reversal of trends in US living standards during the 12-year reign of the Republican Party. By the early 1990s median family incomes had dropped to their level of the late 1970s, the portion of the population living in poverty had risen significantly, and wealth and income inequality had shot up to levels not seen since the 1930s. Perhaps the most telling statistic was that by 1991, more than one out of every five children was defined as poor.[3]

Global Rollback

The same forces, many suspected, were at work in both the North and the South, producing similar consequences for poor and working people everywhere. When the Los Angeles riots broke out in May 1992, many saw the event as one of a kind with the anti-IMF and food riots that had broken out earlier in the Third World, in Santo Domingo, Caracas, and São Paulo. All were essentially poor peoples' responses to a wrenching process to which economists and technocrats had given the euphemism 'adjustment.'

This book constitutes an effort to confirm analytically and empirically the widely shared sense that the collapse of the South and the greater insecurity in the working and living conditions of most people in the North were consequences of the same thing – a sweeping strategy of global economic rollback unleashed by Northern political and corporate elites to consolidate corporate hegemony in the home economy and shore up the North's domination of the international economy.

Central to this process was the leadership of a highly ideological Republican regime in Washington, which abandoned the grand strategy of 'containment liberalism' abroad and the New Deal modus vivendi at home. Aside from defeating communism, Reaganism in practice was guided by three other strategic concerns. The first was the resubordination of the South within a US-dominated global economy. The second was the rolling back of the challenge to US economic interests from the NICs, or 'newly industrializing countries,' and from Japan. The third was the dismantling of the New Deal 'social contract' between big capital, big labor, and big government which both Washington and Wall Street saw as the key constraint on corporate America's ability to compete against both the NICs and Japan.

Conspiracy or Ideology?

It is worthwhile to pause briefly here to consider if this argument is tantamount to advancing a conspiracy theory of recent history. Far from it. The last image this analysis wishes to convey is that of corporate and political elites plotting at the White House or in Manhattan highrises to impose global adjustment. This is *never* the way that major shifts in national policy come about.

What usually occurs is a much more complex social process in which *ideology* mediates between interests and policy. An ideology is a belief-system – a set of theories, beliefs, and myths with some internal coherence – that seeks to universalize the interests of one social sector to the whole community. In market ideology, for instance, freeing market forces from state restraints is said to work to the good not only of business, but also to that of the whole community.

Transmitted through social institutions such as universities, corporations, churches or parties, an ideology is internalized by large numbers of people, but especially by members of the social groups whose interests it principally expresses. An ideology thus informs the actions of many individuals and groups, but it becomes a significant force only when certain conditions coincide. For example, radical free-market ideas as an alternative to the post-War Keynesian 'social contract' had been floating around for quite some time before the 1980s, particularly among certain cultural elites ensconced in universities. However, market ideology became a dominant force only when a political elite which espoused it ascended to state power on the back of an increasingly conservative middle-class social base, at the same time that the corporate establishment was deserting the

liberal Keynesian consensus in its favor, because of the changed circumstances of international economic competition.

Thus, the wide sharing of the assumptions of free-market ideology
by cultural, state, and economic elites during the Reagan–Bush era
obviated the need for crude conspiracy. Indeed, not only were these
assumptions shared, they were widely propagated and fervently
believed by ideologues as the solution to the problems of both the
United States and the world. Of course, the translation from ideology
to policy was affected by differences of opinion on the efficacy of
specific policies, differences between hardliners and pragmatists,
and differences occasioned by personal ambitions. But for the most
part, the broad thrust of championing private enterprise, rolling
back communism and the insurgent South, eliminating state intervention in the economy, reducing government-supported safety
nets, and 'freeing labor markets' by dismantling unionism were all
aims shared by the dominant state, cultural, and corporate elites.

There was not, however, a full correspondence between ideology
and interests. Free-market ideology has an intellectual consistency
and coherence that leads it to champion competition over oligopoly.
Here is where the promotion of interests took precedence over
ideological integrity during the Reagan–Bush era. Deregulation, or
unfettering the marketplace, became a means not of breaking up
oligopolies but of doing away with the obstacles in the way of
corporate mergers and acquisitions that led to an even higher concentration of corporate wealth. Letting the market weed out inefficient
producers was a principle that was left by the wayside as Washington
increased subsidies to US farmers and tightened quotas on imports
of NIC-produced textiles and garments in order to protect US cloth
manufacturers.

Dismantling the Activist State

Ultimately then, the strategic coherence of the Republican policies
was provided not by their pro-competition principles but by their
anti-statist and pro-corporate thrust: the elimination of state supports
for production in the South and the NICs and the reduction of state
restraints on corporate activity in the United States. From the
viewpoint of the free-market vanguard which dominated Washington,
state intervention via protectionism and foreign investment restrictions prevented US capital from fully penetrating Third World
economies; aggressive state support for domestic firms in the NICs
militated against the creation of a 'level playing field' for US corpo-

rations; and exorbitant taxation of the private sector and en
ment of environmental and labor standards prevented US capital from
becoming competitive with the formidable Japanese.

In the South, the debt crisis of 1982 served as the opening for the
imposition of structural adjustment programs – via the World Bank
and the International Monetary Fund – that sought to roll back the
state from economic life. The aim was to weaken domestic
entrepreneurial groups by eliminating protectionist barriers to imports
from the North and by lifting restrictions on foreign investment; to
overwhelm the weak legal barriers protecting labor from capital;
and to integrate the local economy more tightly into the North-
dominated world economy.

Against the NICs, trade policy was the choice weapon. While
Washington's immediate goal was to rectify trade imbalances by
reducing NIC exports to the US and prying open NIC markets, its
strategic objective – so clear in its treatment of South Korea, the NIC
par excellence – was to dismantle the system of state intervention
and support that had enabled NIC producers, following the 'Japanese
model,' to compete successfully against American corporations not
only in world markets but in the US market itself.

In the US, 'getting government off the back of business' took the
form of a radical reduction of tax rates on the rich, removal of state
restraints on corporate mergers and acquisitions, and weaker enforcement of environmental standards. Above all, it meant giving
government support to aggressive corporate efforts to bust unions
and weaken labor's resistance to the drive to achieve competitiveness by reducing wages and benefits, 'downsizing' the domestic
workforce, and transferring manufacturing operations to cheap labor
areas in the Third World.

Ironically, however, a Republican regime pledged to arrest US
decline ended up accelerating it by pursuing domestic policies that
might have strengthened US military power and produced economic
growth in the short term, but that weakened the US techno-industrial
capability in the long term. One of these strategic blunders was the
massive deficit spending on defense, which made the US the world's
top debtor country, especially to Japan, America's main competitor.
Another was the eschewing of state-led economic planning in the
name of market principles, putting the economic future of the US
in the hands of corporations that were mainly interested in short-
term profitability. A third strategic error was made in allowing the
corporations to squander, with their anti-labor strategy of regaining

competitiveness, the United State's key resource in global competition: its human capital.

Barbarians at the Gates

Having dismantled the New Deal mechanisms for social peace at home and abandoned the strategy of liberal containment abroad, the US, under the Reagan and Bush administrations, was reduced to punitive strategies to deal with rising domestic discontent and growing resistance in the South. Indeed, the Southern policies of all the key Northern governments on the eve of the twenty-first century are marked by similar features. These include continued support for structural adjustment in the Third World; creation of a new Berlin Wall to prevent the entry of refugees fleeing the devastation of the South; exploitation of tribal fears of racial and ethnic minorities to deflect domestic attention away from the structural causes of economic distress; and demonization of Southern figures or institutions, such as Islam, as the new enemy in the post-Cold War era.

Although a new Democratic administration has ascended to power in Washington, hopes that it will break with the policies in place are likely to be misplaced. Continuing support for structural adjustment, an even more aggressive trade policy, the June 1993 bombing of Iraq ordered by President Bill Clinton, and support for the North American Free Trade Agreement (NAFTA) designed to consolidate a cheap-labor preserve south of the border indicate continuity rather than the promise of change. 'New Democratic Thinking' may well be less ideological, more pragmatic, more technocratic in approach than Reaganism, but it does not appear to question the basic strategy of local and global economic restructuring chosen by US corporations, nor is it incompatible with the anti-South military strategy that is consolidating within the defense establishment.

Not surprisingly, the dark vision of the twenty-first century as an era of North–South polarization between privileged white citizens and colored barbarian hordes, or between the Christian West and the 'Islamic-Confucian Connection', has begun to take hold in the writings of Northern intellectuals. Will they be prophetic? Or can progressive forces still successfully mount an effective movement for an alternative future based on the reality that, for the most part, the peoples of the North and South share the same condition of being victims of the same counter-revolution that serves the interests of a global minority?

2

Challenge from the South

For many, there was the hope born of success in their liberation struggles. Everywhere there was talk of equality and progress ... It is important to remember this period of progress and its atmosphere of hope now, when there is deep pessimism in much of the Third World about the prospects of economic development.

—South Commission, *The Challenge to the South*
(New York: Oxford University Press, 1990)

Southern Sunrise

The 1960s and 1970s were years that saw significant gains for the Third World, or South. National independence movements came to power or were institutionalized in Cuba, Mozambique, Angola, Guinea-Bissau, Vietnam, Laos, Kampuchea, Nicaragua, Iran, and Zimbabwe. Moreover, stimulated by development strategies in which the state played a central role, Southern economies grew. Latin America's gross domestic product (GDP) rose by an average of 5 per cent per annum between 1960 and 1982, while Africa's climbed by an average of 4 per cent. Of course, the Asia-Pacific region, with its much-touted 'tiger economies' (Taiwan, South Korea, Hong Kong, and Singapore), was the Third World's star player, with regional GDP registering an average increase of 7 per cent a year.[1]

In the three decades after 1950, the South's rate of economic growth was not only higher than the North's during the same period, it was also higher than the rate for the developed countries in their early stages of development.[2] With per capita income doubling between 1950 and 1980, the proportion of people living in absolute poverty, though not their numbers, was reduced.[3] In Latin America, for instance, the share of families below the poverty line defined by the Economic Commission for Latin America decreased from 51 to 40 per cent in just 10 years, 1960–70, while the proportion below the 'line of destitution' dropped from 26 to 19 per cent.[4] The growth locomotive pulled not only the relatively less deprived countries of Latin America but even the poorest countries too, many of them in

7

Africa, providing testimony, according to the South Commission, 'of the remarkable results that can be achieved through public policy and social action, despite low levels of national income.'[5]

True, the pattern of growth in the South was not ideal. For instance, inefficiency often marked the operation of state enterprises and protected industries, and environmental destabilization was usually a by-product of industrial growth. These facts, however, must be seen in context. Inefficiency did not, for the most part stifle growth, and state-led or state-assisted capitalism was critical in enhancing national control over the economy. And when one assesses the environmental impact of the efforts of Third World countries to industrialize, it must be borne in mind that this was puny compared to the national and international ecological consequences of the high-consumption driven, highly wasteful economic strategies pursued by the Northern economies during the same period.

State and the Market in the Third World

In the newly independent societies of the South, private ownership of land, resources, and enterprises was the rule, and economic exchange was largely mediated by the market. However, government intervention in economic life was pervasive, and the state had a strategic role in economic transformation. Nowhere was this more evident than in industry, which was actively and often aggressively promoted by the state through strategic planning, development finance, trade protectionism, and public investment in vital enterprises.[6]

Contrary to conservative doctrine, the prominence of the state in post-colonial economic development did not stem from a usurpation of the role of private enterprise; rather, it was a response to the weakness of private industrial interests. '[T]he state,' observes one analyst, 'became a surrogate for private enterprise that could drive modernization without challenging ... entrenched interests – indeed, would continue to protect them – and without turning the country completely over to foreign interests.'[7] Instead of subverting the private sector, public enterprises and public spending 'crowded in' private investment: that is, they increased the profitability of the private sector by 'nationalizing risk' in strategic sectors such as energy and infrastructure. In such hybrid 'state-assisted capitalist regimes,' which were commonplace in Latin America and East Asia, the synergy between the public and private sectors 'carried capital accumulation to a higher level than would have arisen spontaneously out of the free market.'[8]

Diversity and Unity

While the emerging South was a mix of conservative, liberal, state socialist, communist, and state-assisted capitalist economic regimes, most shared a common feeling of having been exploited by the North, a common goal of 'catching up' with the rich countries, a common perspective that government leadership was central in economic development, and a common belief that cooperation among Southern governments would play a decisive role in rectifying the global imbalance between North and South.

The East–West conflict and domestic class politics did split the South on key issues. For example, Brazil's leadership was fervently anti-communist, while Cuba saw itself as the spearhead of socialism in the Americas. Yet Brazil and Cuba, radical Libya and conservative Saudi Arabia, anti-imperialist Vietnam and anti-communist Indonesia could unite around the vision of a global redistribution of economic power enshrined in the program of the 'New International Economic Order' (NIEO) adopted by a special session of the United Nations (UN) General Assembly in 1974. Tentatively united by this sense of being structurally and historically disadvantaged vis-à-vis the North, governments with disparate positions on many issues could nevertheless come together to express a common agenda in such fora as the Non-Aligned Movement, the United Nations Conference on Trade and Development (UNCTAD), and the Group of 77.

The rhetoric of solidarity seemed on the verge of becoming reality in the early 1970s, when the Organization of Petroleum Exporting Countries (OPEC) managed finally to seize control of the pricing of oil and moved to increase its share of profits which had formerly been largely monopolized by the Western oil corporations. OPEC's success in quadrupling the price of oil in late 1973 triggered similar attempts by Third World countries to create cartels in bauxite, tin, and other raw materials as well as in agricultural commodities. Hopeful that OPEC would throw its weight behind these moves and thrilled by the decisive Vietnamese victory over the United States, many Third World governments felt they were indeed on the threshold of a new global political and economic order in the mid-1970s.

3
Liberalism and Containment

> The Communist threat against the free nations ... and the overriding poverty and lack of development ... These are the twin and related objectives which the foreign aid program seeks to meet.
>
> —W. Averell Harriman, New Deal and Cold War figure, quoted in Bernard Nossiter, *The Global Struggle for More* (New York: Harper and Row, 1987, p. 116)

The rise of the Third World coincided with the hegemony of Cold War liberals in Washington, DC ensconced principally in the Democratic Party, but with fellow travellers in the East Coast wing of the Republican Party, these elements were central to the design and institutionalization of the grand strategy of containment directed against Soviet communism.

Liberalism and Anti-Communism: The Peculiar Mix

Containment liberalism[1] was anti-communist in foreign affairs but liberal in domestic policy. This translated into the New Deal and neo-New Deal *sozialepolitik* of high government spending, capitalist expansion, and growing real incomes for labor that underpinned a modus vivendi between big government, big business, and big labor.

Anti-communism and liberalism were also the two elements that came to define the stance of the liberals toward the countries emerging from colonialism, which they came to regard as critical battlegrounds of the Cold War. While they believed force to be the decisive arbiter in this conflict, they were convinced also that growing Third World markets were in the interest of US capital and, that to be successful, armed counter-insurgency had to be accompanied by a degree of economic stability, if not prosperity. Aid to the Third World played a central role in this strategy, for it was, in the view of Paul Hoffman, a key figure in the post-war foreign policy establishment, 'an instrument to preserve democracy and capitalism by providing stability and the foundation of economic growth.'[2]

10

The liberal approach to managing the rising South was evident in the circumstances surrounding the creation of the International Development Association (IDA), the World Bank's 'soft-loan' arm, in 1960. The IDA was created as a substitute for the Special United Nations Fund for Development (SUNFED) proposed by the developing countries in the late 1950s. As Eugene Black, president of the World Bank, admitted, 'The International Development Association was really an idea to offset the urge for Sunfed.'[3] While Washington liberals like Black viewed the IDA as a key instrument in their plans for limited redistribution of global wealth, they also wanted to control the process, which they accomplished by making the Association an affiliate of the World Bank rather than an agency of the UN.[4]

The same approach marked the establishment of the regional banks, the African Development Bank, the Inter-American Development Bank, and the Asian Development Bank – all of which guaranteed Northern hegemony by allocating influence according to the size of capital subscriptions, not membership.

Other key reformist initiatives included the establishment of the IMF's Compensatory Financing Facility (CFF) to assist Third World countries in managing foreign exchange crises created by sharp falls in the prices of the primary commodities they exported, and the General System of Preferences (GSP), which provided preferential treatment to selected manufactured exports from developing nations.

All these multilateral institutions and agreements were part of the same strategy of US-managed development that produced the more publicized Alliance for Progress and the Peace Corps during the Kennedy era. By promising development cum limited social reform, containment liberalism hoped to take the wind out of the sails not only of communist movements but also of Third World nationalists such as Sukarno of Indonesia and Nasser of Egypt, who were demanding fundamental changes in North–South relations.

Containment liberalism was pragmatic when it came to dealing with issues that included protectionism and the role of state intervention in Third World countries. While it usually drew the line when it came to the nationalization of US firms in the Third World, as it did when Salvador Allende's Unidad Popular government nationalized the Kennecott and Anaconda copper mines in Chile in 1971, containment liberalism did not respond in a doctrinaire fashion to protected markets and state-led development in the South. More important than their internal economic structures was where Third World countries stood on the question of combatting 'communist subversion' internally and communist expansion globally, which was Washington's primary concern during the Cold War. Nowhere was the subordination of economic doctrine to the priority of the anti-communist alliance more pronounced than when it came to front-line states of the Cold War, such as Taiwan and South Korea. So long as they remained allies in the anti-communist crusade, both Democratic and Republican administrations in Washington could live with the closed markets and restrictive foreign investment laws which the military–technocrat elites maintained in these economies.[5]

There was another reason too for official Washington's ambivalence. This stemmed from the origins of the US post-war economy in the Keynesian political economy of the New Deal, which had relied on state intervention to 'correct' the failures of the market. Indeed, the field of development economics that was born in the 1950s and 1960s envisioned a central role for government in economic 'take-off.' As Roger Stone notes, 'As was Kennedy-era economics in the United States, the early World Bank model is often described as 'neo-Keynesian' in recognition of its emphasis on government planning and job creation in the context of a free economy.'[6]

Kennedy's secretary of defense, Robert McNamara, reaffirmed a basic tenet of containment liberalism when he asserted in 1964 that 'the foreign aid program is the best weapon we have to insure that our own men in uniform need not go into combat.'[7] But contrary to public assurances by McNamara and other Cold War liberals, US troops did go into combat in Vietnam in the early 1960s. Vietnam, however, was more than a military expedition. It was also an experiment in the liberal strategy of containment, where military engagement of the guerrillas was accompanied by an attempt to engineer a capitalist revolution by promoting reform of a corrupt feudal system of rule, urging land redistribution, pouring in aid, and spreading new technologies such as hybrid, high-yielding seeds.[8] By delivering economic growth, this development process, it was hoped, would reduce the attractiveness of the communist program and eventually lead to political stability.

The US right, which favored a total military solution with no pretense at reform, thus saw Vietnam not simply as a political and military defeat but also as the failure of the liberal strategy of economic containment. It was doubly incensed by what it regarded as Vietnam's 'demonstration effect' on the rest of the Third World. For US conservatives, there was a linear progression from Vietnam's successful defiance of the United States to the Arab oil embargo in 1973 and the declaration of the NIEO in 1974.

But although its political component was discredited by Vietnam, liberal containment as an economic strategy continued to retain its credibility in the 1970s. For the most part, the Republican presidents

Richard Nixon and Gerald Ford maintained the economic policies toward the South that had been followed by preceding Democratic administrations. Indeed, the economic approach of containment liberalism obtained a new lease of life with Robert McNamara's transfer to the World Bank after his disastrous stint as manager of the Southeast Asian war. Containment liberalism McNamara-style rested on the belief that 'the poor could gain a larger share of the national wealth without political and social upheaval or without seriously depriving local elites.'[9] However, this could only be accomplished with significant infusions of foreign capital, especially aid. Thus McNamara raised World Bank lending to the Third World from an average of US$2.7 billion a year in the early 1970s to $8.7 billion by 1978. By the time he left office in 1981, the Bank's yearly loan commitments had reached $12 billion.

The Bank's vastly expanded program was accompanied by the elaboration of a global anti-poverty program directed at the 700–800 million people, or 35–40 per cent of the world's 2 billion people, who were defined as living in 'absolute poverty.'[10] The principal targets were small farmers, who were to be reached with rural development programs that brought together rural road construction, smallholder credit systems, and Green Revolution technology. By upgrading the 'productivity of the poor' and allowing the benefits of growth to flow instead of trickle down to the bottom of Third World societies, McNamara hoped to expand and consolidate *kulak*, or smallholder, strata that would act as a barrier to radical social change in the countryside.

Another major feature of the McNamara program was its imposition from above. Eliminating poverty was viewed as an engineering or management problem, a task that could best be performed by technocrats or the managers of the national economy. Since in key Third World countries, technocrats had teamed up with military or dictatorial elites to manage social change, it was not suprising that Bank programs became part and parcel of authoritarian modernization schemes. Early on, McNamara gave top priority to expanding the Bank's programs in Indonesia and Brazil, both of which were then ruled by repressive governments. And soon after Marcos installed a dictatorship in 1972, the Philippines became a 'country of concentration' for World Bank funds.[11] By the late 1970s, in fact, five of the top eight recipients of Bank loans were authoritarian regimes. The alliance of liberalism with repression was, however, consistent with McNamara and the American liberals' experience in Vietnam, where they had sought to use first a feudal despot, Ngo Dinh Diem, and then generals, as agents of a defensive, capitalist modernization.

After resigning as US secretary of defense, Robert McNamara became World Bank president in 1968. McNamara presided over a sharp increase in bank lending to the Third World under his policy of liberal containment. (Photo: World Bank)

The infusion of multilateral bank funds went hand-in-hand with the much larger infusion of credits from Western private banks. While the private banks recycled the billions of OPEC 'petrodollars' deposited with them after the 1973 oil price rise as loans to Third World countries, with an eye to turning a profit at a time when credit demand was depressed in their home economies, containment liberals perceived an additional, political payoff: these credits, like

World Bank aid, would defuse dissent and ward off radical revolution in strategic countries allied to the West. Not surprisingly, despite increasing fears expressed in the late 1970s about the capacity of Third World states to service their debts, McNamara saw the acceleration of private lending to the Third World as 'neither surprising nor undesirable.'[12] The World Bank's key clients were also the biggest debtors to the commercial banks, and foreign credit to these countries was, as debt expert Karin Lissakers describes it, 'the glue that held together fragile political coalitions of urban workers, a growing middle class of mostly public sector employees, and the military ... Foreign money enabled governments to survive without resolving fundamental political and economic inequities in their countries.'[13]

This political economy of high growth cum high foreign indebtedness rested on a peculiar social contract in which

rapid economic growth financed with foreign credit was the trade-off for limited political freedom or outright repression. And foreign loans helped pay for government subsidies that were to compensate the economically disenfranchised who did not benefit directly from the expansion. Holding down the price of beans and rice, bread, gasoline, and public transportation by subsidizing producers was politically more expedient than trying to correct glaring inequities in income distribution through land and wage reforms, education reform, and progressive taxation.[14]

The Collapse of Containment Liberalism

By the late 1970s, however, even the economic program of liberal containment strategy was under fire, for it had not produced what it had promised to deliver: security for Western interests in the South through the cooptation of Third World elites.

While professing anti-communism, governing elites throughout the Third World gave in to popular pressure, abetted by local industrial interests, to tighten up on foreign investment. Nowhere did this trend spark more apprehension among American business people than in two countries which were considered enormously strategic by US multinational firms. In Brazil, where foreign-owned firms accounted for half of total manufacturing sales,[15] the military–technocrat regime, invoking national security considerations, moved in the late 1970s to reserve the strategic information sector to local industries, provoking bitter denunciation from IBM (International Business Machines) and other US computer firms.[16] In Mexico, where foreign firms accounted for nearly 30 per cent of manufacturing output,[17] legal actions and threats of disinvestment by the powerful US drug industry followed the government's program for the pharmaceutical industry, which proposed no-patent policies, promotion of generic medicines, local development of raw materials, price controls, discriminatory incentives for local firms, and controls on foreign investment.[18]

The World Bank building, Washington, DC. (Photo: World Bank)

Disturbing though these actions were, they could not compare in their impact with OPEC's second 'oil shock' in 1979. Despite the fact that the Western oil companies were passing on the oil price increases to consumers in order to preserve their enormous profit margins, to many Americans OPEC became the symbol of the South: an irresponsible gang that was bent on using its monopoly to bring the West to its knees. Although OPEC was not dominated by communists or by radical nationalists like Libya's Khadafy but by US allies such as Saudi Arabia, Kuwait, and Venezuela, its 'oil weapon' evoked more apprehension than the nuclear arms of the communist foes. Indeed, the oil cartel was feared as the precursor of a unified Southern bloc controlling most strategic commodities.

The North–South cleavage began to supersede the East–West divide in the American consciousness. Joined to the perception of US paralysis during the Iran hostage crisis in 1979 and 1980, this exaggerated fear of the South's economic clout probably contributed more to the defeat of the liberal Jimmy Carter and Ronald Reagan's coming to power in November 1980 than the familiar communist threat did.

4

Reaganism and Rollback

Government does not solve problems. It subsidizes them.

> —Ronald Reagan, quoted in Lou Cannon,
> *President Reagan: Role of a Lifetime*
> (New York: Simon and Schuster, 1991)

Free enterprise works because, like democracy, it gives real power to the people.

> —Margaret Thatcher, quoted in *The Nation*
> (Bangkok), Sept. 7, 1993

[Foreign aid] is the source of the North–South conflict, not its solution.

> —Peter Bauer and Basil Yamey, economists, 'Foreign Aid:
> What is at Stake?,' *The Public Interest*, Summer 1992

The Reagan administration came to power with an agenda to discipline the Third World. While the East–West confrontation became the subject of President Reagan's most dramatic pronouncements, to many members of the new Washington crowd the North–South conflict was just as critical as the East–West divide, breaking OPEC was as much of a priority as rolling back Soviet communism, and McNamara liberals at the World Bank were just as villainous as McGovernites at the State Department.

Diverse traditions fed into the philosophy and posture of triumphant Reaganism, but central to it were ideological strains associated with the mid-western and western wings of the Republican Party from which both Barry Goldwater and Ronald Reagan sprang.[1] These elements of the party, whose views resonated with the interests of conservative rural communities, the suburban middle class, and non-East Coast business, saw the United States as being besieged on two fronts: internationally by communism and internally by New Deal liberalism.

The Worldview of Reaganism

To them, the liberal democratic tradition of big government, social welfare, and support for labor went against the American grain of individual freedom and free markets and represented creeping socialism. At the same time, they regarded containment, which had been formulated by liberal democrats, as a form of appeasing international communism by surrendering the struggle to liberate those living under communist rule. By compromising with both the New Deal and with containment, the eastern, liberal wing of the party had ceased to be the voice of true Republicanism.

It should come as no surprise then, that the alternative worldview around which these sectors of the Republican Party united was one of 'rollback.' This was a strategy that advocated, on the international front, rolling back communism from Eastern Europe, China, and eventually the Soviet Union, and, on the domestic arena, rolling back big government and big labor from domestic economic life.

These two thrusts of rollback – against international threats to US power and against government intervention in the economy – were reproduced in the Reaganites' interpretation of the challenge from the South and in their elaboration of a strategy for dealing with it.

The Reaganite View of the South

Right-wing think-tanks such as the Heritage Foundation took the lead in promoting the Southern threat and they painted this in distinctly conspiratorial terms. In the view of the Foundation, during the 1970s the South had unfolded a systematic strategy to undermine the North:

> At the Algiers nonaligned summit of 1973, the Group of 77 urged political unity to gain economic power. The participants demanded extensive economic concessions by Western nations. The following year they moved their campaign to the UN General Assembly, and approved the 'Declaration on Establishment of a New International Economic Order' and the 'Charter of Economic Rights and Duties of States.' These resolutions were the philosophical framework for a decade-long assault on the West in pursuit of a New International Economic Order (NIEO).[2]

The developing countries, continued the Foundation critique, devoted 'enormous time and resources to spreading the NIEO ideology throughout the UN system and beyond. Virtually no UN agencies and bureaus have been spared.'[3]

What did the South want? Practically everything:

> A key element of NIEO's demands is financial redistribution: inter-
> national taxation, increased foreign assistance, the right to
> expropriate private foreign assets, commodity price protection, and
> commercial preferences regarding shipping and trade generally.
> Technological redistribution, through mandatory transfer of
> industrial, seabed, space, and pharmaceutical technology has been
> another NIEO tenet.[4]

Especially threatening to the Foundation was the effort of the
Third World to 'redistribute natural resources' by

> bringing the seabed, space, and Antarctica under their control
> through the Law of the Sea Treaty, the Agreement Governing
> Activities of States on the Moon and Other Celestial Bodies (called
> the 'Moon Treaty'), and an ongoing UN study and debate over
> Antarctica. Malaysian Prime Minister Mahathir Bin Mohamad,
> the principal architect of the effort to get the UN to claim Antarctica,
> told the General Assembly 'all the unclaimed wealth of this earth'
> is the 'common heritage of mankind,' and therefore subject to the
> political control of the Third World.[5]

Where the South had not sought legal title to the world's resources,
it had attempted 'to regulate them':

> Private business data flows are under attack internationally and
> by individual Third World countries; proposals for strict control
> of the international pharmaceutical trade are pending before more
> than one UN body; other international agencies are drafting restric-
> tive codes of conduct for multinational corporations; and UNESCO
> has proposed international restraints on the press.[6]

The villain of the piece was Third World government. In the eyes
of the Reaganites, whatever their formal political orientation, most
Third World governments – with the exception of Chile and colonial
Hong Kong – were uniformly interventionist and uniformly economic
failures. They had 'mismanaged their economies simply by trying to
manage them.'[7] This mismanagement consisted of imposing restrictions on the natural operation of free-market forces, such as
protectionist mechanisms for domestic enterprises that deprived
consumers of quality foreign products; maintenance of overvalued
exchange rates that discouraged exports; foreign investment controls

that promoted inefficient production; and price policies that discouraged food production.

The South's demand-for redistribution was actually aimed at making up for the failure of the Southern states to produce wealth. Thus, entertaining this demand by increasing aid flows would merely exacerbate economic decline rather than arresting it: 'while it does little or nothing to promote development, aid can relieve immediate shortages, especially of consumer goods and imports. This makes it easier for governments to conceal temporarily from their populations the worst effects of damaging policies.'[8]

More broadly, argued conservative analysts Peter Bauer and Basil Yamey in an influential article, aid

> increases the money, patronage, and power of the recipient governments, and thereby their grip over the rest of society. It thus promotes a disastrous politicization of life in the Third World ... When social and economic life is extensively politicized, people's livelihood or even their economic and physical survival comes to depend on political and administrative decisions. This result promotes conflict ... This sequence diverts energy and attention from productive activity to the political arena; and the direction of people's activities is necessarily a crucial determinant of economic performance.[9]

In sum, 'not only is foreign aid patently not required for development, it is, in actual fact, much more likely to obstruct it.'[10] Moreover, foreign aid 'is the source of the the North–South conflict, not its solution.'[11]

More broadly, the Reaganite critique disagreed with containment liberalism's premise that a more prosperous South would work in the the interest of the US by promoting stability. The South had, indeed, gained more wealth, but it was at the expense of the North. Moreover, the liberal strategy had not purchased global stability. Containment liberals had not only encouraged communist expansion by their hesitation to use force in a decisive way in Vietnam, but through generous aid policies they had appeased nationalist forces and selfish Third World elites who were intent on destroying the North's global economic hegemony.

Indeed, many people in the new administration believed that the interests of the North were fundamentally antagonistic to those of the South, and that the task of the moment was to repair the damage through firm policies aimed at rolling back the South and resubordinating the increasingly unmanageable Third World within a

Meeting of North–South world leaders at Cancun, Mexico, October 1981. Reagan is seated at far left. This summit was intended to lead to a new stage in the North–South dialogue. Actually, it inaugurated a decade of debt and decline. (Reagan Presidential Library)

US-dominated world economic system. In October 1981, Ronald Reagan travelled to Cancun, Mexico, to attend the much-heralded economic summit that was expected to lead to a new stage in North–South relations. Cancun, instead, turned out be the prelude to a global economic counter-revolution carried out in the name of the free market.

The Vulnerable South

For those in the Reagan administration who favored a confrontational strategy toward the South, the international economic conditions developing in the early 1980s provided propitious circumstances for launching an economic offensive. First of all, despite the seeming united front it had displayed during the second major hike in oil prices in 1979, OPEC in fact experienced deep divisions within its ranks in the early 1980s. There were splits between radical regimes like Iran, which wanted to use oil as a weapon against the West, and conservative US allies such as Saudi Arabia; between 'income maximizers', including Iraq, and 'market-share maximizers' like the Saudis.[12] Furthermore, the development and accelerated exploitation of oil fields that were not in OPEC's control, such as those in the North Sea and Alaska, significantly weakened the cartel's grip on oil prices.

Moreover, through skillful diplomacy, the US had been able in the late 1970s to detach OPEC from the efforts of other groups of Third World countries to form effective price-controlling cartels in bauxite, tin, and other raw materials. When Third World governments flocked to Paris in 1975 to confront the North at the crucial Conference on International Economic Cooperation (CIEC), many came with the expectation that the OPEC producers would stand with them to demand a comprehensive deal on a wide range of commodities. But the Saudis had been bought off: in return for allowing Saudi Arabia to purchase US treasury bills with the exact amounts kept secret, the Saudis agreed not to allow oil to be used as a weapon in the commodity conflict. The unspoken working compromise was that the Saudis and other Arab OPEC producers were 'free to determine the price of oil so long as the supply of oil was not interrupted and oil revenues were not used to weaken the existing economic system.'[13] The deal exposed the fragility behind the South's rhetoric of solidarity, revealing that the interests of the oil elites were more congruent with those of the industrial–financial elites of the North.

The second economic condition of the early 1980s was that, with the onset of recession in the industrial North, the prices of raw materials from the South were dropping to their lowest level since the 1930s. With many Third World countries dependent on one or two commodities to gain foreign exchange, the drop in prices meant that their ability to service their mounting foreign debts was severely constrained. The plight of many economies dependent on commodity exports was also exacerbated by advances in biotechnology and materials science, which resulted in the creation of substitutes for raw materials sourced from the Third World, such as corn syrup for sugar or enzyme-engineered 'cocoa butter equivalents' for cocoa.[14]

The third condition, and perhaps the Third World's most vulnerable point, was that it was skating on thin ice financially. It had US$700 billion worth of debts to American, European, and Japanese banks, which had competed intensely with one another to make loans to Southern governments in order to make profits from the huge sums of OPEC money deposited with them after the first oil price shock. Bank lending to the Third World had lost the least modicum of restraint under Citicorp chairman Walter Wriston's doctrine that, unlike individuals, 'A country does not go bankrupt.'[15] By the late 1970s neither borrowers nor lenders were so sure of this, as each percentage increase in international interest rates added hundreds of millions of dollars to the yearly debt service of countries which had agreed to loans set not at fixed but at variable interest rates. Not surprisingly, Third World debtors were increasingly locked into a desperate game of borrowing from one set of lenders to pay off another set.

Harnessing the World Bank

Aid policy became the key weapon in the Reagan administration's disciplining of the South. For most Reaganites, there appeared to be a consensus that aid was mainly a political instrument, one that should be deployed primarily to bolster the position of the US in international power politics. Indeed, over the Reagan years, non-military bilateral aid tied to security goals grew in real terms by over 80 per cent, while development assistance and food aid declined.[16] The top five recipients of 'Economic Support Funds' between 1981 and 1986 were all countries that were regarded as strategic to the US in either the anti-communist struggle (El Salvador, Pakistan, and Turkey) or the anti-Third World campaign (Israel, Egypt).

Bilateral assistance disbursed by the Agency for International Development, it was argued, should be conditioned on the adoption of policies which promoted the free market and channelled to support the growth of private enterprises in the Third World. Some argued for reducing the US government's role in humanitarian assistance and leaving this task largely to private entities, because 'judgments as to moral responsibility for the world's poor are best left to private individuals and organizations, not government officials.'[17]

US aid channelled through multilateral organizations, which accounted for about a fifth of all US aid disbursements by the late 1970s, was the most controversial proposal. Some Reaganites proposed that it should be phased out, or at the least not increased, because 'the more distant the relationship between the supplier of funds and their user, the more likely that they will be used ineffectively.'[18] Thus the World Bank, with its US$12 billion budget, became the principal focus of the Reaganites' program for putting the South in its place. While some would have been happy to withold US funds from an institution they regarded as a key promoter of statist economic policies in the Third World, more pragmatic conservatives in the Treasury Department, who oversaw Bank operations, came to view the Bank as a useful, if not central, instrument in their effort to discipline the Third World.

Reading the writing on the wall, Robert McNamara, the classical containment liberal, resigned in 1981. With McNamara gone and his key aides (including the Pakistani Mahbub Ul-Haq, head of the elite Planning and Program Review Department and the brains behind the Bank's anti-poverty thrust) following him, the Bank's 'basic needs' program withered on the vine. In McNamara's place the administration, using the time-honored US 'right' to fill the Bank's top job with an American citizen, nominated a pliable personality, A.W. ('Tom') Clausen, the former head of the Bank of America. And, in the mid-eighties, the post was filled by an even more congenial sort – ex-Republican congressman Barber Conable. The way was clear for the Reaganites to mold the 6,000-person agency to push their rollback agenda.

The first salvo in this campaign was the decision to cut the US' promised contribution to the 1982 replenishment of the International Development Association (IDA), the Bank's soft-loan window, by US$300 million. This led the other advanced countries to cut their own contributions, resulting in the soft-loan agency receiving $1 billion less than it originally expected. Since IDA loans were granted on concessional terms to the poorest countries, – for example, India, other Southeast Asian countries, and African countries – the move served as a forceful signal from the Reaganites that the US and its allies were 'cutting off the dole.' This was the first step in a process of changing the criterion for the allocation of IDA funds from countries that needed them because they were defined as poor (having a per capita income of US$400 or less), to those that were regarded as 'making the greatest efforts to restructure their economies.'[19]

Selling SALs

Then, the US pushed the Bank to shift more of its resources from traditional project lending to 'structural adjustment' lending. Formulated in the last years of the McNamara era, structural adjustment loans (SALs) were more systematically used by the Reagan Treasury Department to blast open Third World economies. SALs were quick-disbursing loans which could be used to relieve a country's balance-of-payments deficit or to repay interest falling due to private banks. But to receive SALs from either the World Bank or the IMF, a government had to agree to undergo a program of thoroughgoing structural adjustment (SAP) which was ostensibly designed to make its economy more efficient and capable of sustained growth.

The conditions usually attached to SALs and their rationale were the following:

- radically reducing government spending, in order to control inflation and reduce the demand for capital inflows from abroad, a measure that in practice translated into cutting spending in health, education, and welfare;
- cutting wages or severely constraining their rise to reduce inflation and make exports more competitive;
- liberalizing imports to make local industry more efficient and instituting incentives for producing for export markets, which were seen both as a source of much-needed foreign exchange and as a more dynamic source of growth than the domestic market;
- removing restrictions on foreign investment in industry and financial services to make the local production of goods and delivery of services more efficient, owing to the presence of foreign competition;
- devaluing the local currency relative to hard currencies like the dollar in order to make exports more competitive; and
- privatizing state enterprises and embarking on radical deregulation in order to promote allocation of resources by the market instead of by government decree.

Acceptance of these conditions was not enough to release a SAL. The recipient had to agree to the Bank and/or the IMF strictly monitoring its compliance with 'targets' agreed upon with Bank technocrats. SALs were released in tranches, so that compliance released a tranche while failure to live up to targets would delay, if not foreclose, further disbursement of loan funds. Since the structural adjustment measures covered so many dimensions of macro economic policy, agreeing to a SAL was virtually turning over control of a country's economy to the World Bank. Indeed, the former executive director for Canada at the Bank testified that

> macropolicy advice incorporated in the SALs touches the very core of the development policy process ... The rate and manner of growth and related societal objectives of the recipient countries are the very stuff of that elusive but important concept called sovereignty.[20]

While World Bank economists tried to sell the SAL as necessary to promote efficiency and sustained growth, Third World leaders accurately perceived from the beginning that the strategic target of structural adjustment programs was the mechanism which the Reaganites had identified as the instrument that made the exercise of economic sovereignty possible and effective: the Third World state.

The Debt Crisis and the Globalization of Adjustment

It should come as no surprise that few governments were eager to receive SALs initially. But with the eruption of the Third World debt crisis in mid-1982, a grand opportunity was presented to the Reaganite agenda of resubordinating the South via structural adjustment. As more and more Third World countries ran into greater difficulties servicing the huge loans made to them by Northern banks in the 1970s, the US and the Bretton Woods institutions, John Sheahan notes, took advantage of 'this period of financial strain to insist that debtor countries remove the government from the economy as the price of getting credit'.[21]

In accordance with guidelines set by the US Treasury Department, the US private banks invariably made World Bank consent a prerequisite for debt rescheduling. And for the debtor countries, the World Bank's seal of approval and its cash, which they desperately needed to make interest payments to the private banks, came dearly. As one Treasury official involved in the debt negotiations with Mexico put it, 'Only countries that commit to market-oriented economic reform will get the [World Bank's] help.'[22]

Structural adjustment was the centerpiece of the Baker Plan, which the Reagan administration proclaimed during the IMF-World Bank meeting in Seoul in 1985. World Bank and IMF funds to assist the indebted countries make their interest payments were promised on condition that they adopted 'economic policies along Reaganomic lines – privatization of state enterprises, an end to subsidies, opening the economies to foreign investment.'[23] In the debtors' view, notes Lissakers, 'the proposed reforms ... went much further than the

US secretary of the Treasury James Baker, author of the Baker Plan, offered indebted countries World Bank and IMF loans in return for structural adjustment of their economies. (Rick Reinhard, Impact Visuals)

standard IMF nostrums on devaluation, reductions in public-sector borrowing requirement and control over the money supply, and decontrol of wages and prices,' and were tantamount to 'putting the national patrimony on the block.'[24] They realized that structural adjustment was, as Sheahan describes it, a program that 'was more extreme than anything that could have been seriously considered at the beginning of the 1960s.'[25]

But they had no choice but to capitulate. By the beginning of 1986, 12 of the 15 debtors designated by then secretary of the Treasury James Baker as top-priority debtors – including Brazil, Mexico, Argentina, and the Philippines – had agreed to SAPs. From 3 per cent of total World Bank lending in 1981, structural adjustment credits rose to 19 per cent in 1986. Five years later, the figure was 25 per cent. By the end of 1992, about 267 SALs had been approved.[26]

Many of the programs that came with these loans were coordinated with the IMF. Originally, IMF 'standby' programs were designed as short-term programs to rectify a country's external account imbalances by forcing the country to eliminate its budget deficit, restrain its money supply, and devalue its currency. However, IMF technocrats came to the opinion that balance-of-payments problems would continue to recur unless more strategic structural reforms designed to expand the role of the market, reduce the role of the state, and integrate a country more fully into the world economy were undertaken. Consequently, IMF standby programs were either extended and designed to incorporate structural reforms as a condition for the Fund's balance-of-payments aid, or they were closely coordinated with the Bank's structural adjustment efforts.

Thus, whereas in the previous division of labor between the two institutions the World Bank was supposed to promote growth and the IMF was expected to monitor financial restraint, their roles now became indistinguishable as both became the enforcers of the North's economic rollback strategy. The unification of the IMF and World Bank treatments came to be known to its patients as 'shock therapy,' or the simultaneous application of short-term stabilization measures and more long-term structural reforms. It was not without reason that adjusting countries came to label the two institutions with derision as the 'Bretton Woods twins.'

Cooperation between the Bank and the Fund was brought to a higher level with the establishment in 1988 of the Structural Adjustment Facility (SAF), set up to coordinate closely the two institutions' surveillance and enforcement activities, especially in sub-Saharan Africa. Out of a total of 47 countries in that region, 36 have undergone SAPs administered by the Bank or the Fund. Since most of these countries have very weak political structures, under the guise of providing aid an IMF–World Bank condominium has been imposed over much of sub-Saharan Africa.

Indeed, with over 70 Third World countries submitting to IMF and World Bank programs in the 1980s, stabilization, structural adjustment, and shock therapy managed from distant Washington became the common condition of the South in that decade. (See Appendix 1 for a list of Third World countries subjected to IMF and World Bank stabilization and structural adjustment programs.) The common objective was the dismantling of the Third World state as an agent of economic development. In 1988, a survey of SAPs carried out by the United Nations Commission for Africa concluded that the essence of the SAPs was the 'reduction/removal of direct state intervention in the productive and distributive sectors of the economy.'[27] Similarly, a retrospective look at the decade of adjustment in a book published by the Inter-American Development Bank in 1992 identified the removal of the state from economic activity as the centerpiece of the ideological perspective that guided the structural reforms of the 1980s:

> In this school of thought, the history of Latin America in the post-war period is the history of a collective error in terms of the economic course chosen, and of the design of the accompanying institutions. To correct that error, the long period during which the public sector has held the center of the economic stage has to be brought to an end, and a radical remedy applied: the withdrawal of the producer State and assisted capitalism, the limiting of the State's reponsibilities to its constitutional commitments, a return to the market for the supply of goods and services, and the removal of obstacles to the emergence of an independent entrepreneurial class.[28]

5
Adjustment: the Record

[E]ven with major adjustment efforts in place, countries do not
fall back on their feet running; they fall into a hole.

> —Rudiger Dornbusch, professor of economics, Massachusetts
> Institute of Technology, quoted in Jacques Polak,
> 'The Changing Nature of IMF Conditionality,
> *Essays in International Finance*, no. 184, September 1991

Thirteen years after the World Bank's first SAP was initiated, the Bank
declared structural adjustment a success in its publication *Global
Economic Prospects and the Developing Countries 1993*. For the rest of
the 1990s, this work asserts,

> developing countries face brighter prospects for growth than in
> the preceding decade. The improved prospects can be attributed
> mainly to the widespread economic reforms these countries have
> adopted, notably privatization, greater openness to trade, reduction
> of fiscal deficits, and commercial debt overhangs.[1]

This is, needless to say, a minority opinion.

A Sorry Record at Best

The empirical record is one of failure, something that is acknowl-
edged by a number of comprehensive studies, including one conducted
by the IMF. Comparing countries which underwent stabilization
and adjustment programs with those which did not, over the period
1973–88, Fund economist Mohsin Khan found that 'the growth rate
is significantly reduced in program countries relative to the change
in non-program countries.'[2] He concluded that while balance of
payments and inflation rates are likely to improve in the first year
of adjustment, these programs 'do involve some cost in terms of a
decline in the growth rate.'[3]

Focusing on the African experience in the 1980s, UNICEF economist
Eva Jespersen assessed a sample of 24 countries which underwent

stabilization and adjustment on three criteria: rate of capital accumulation, diversification of the economic structure measured by the share of manufacturing in GDP; and development of export capabilities. The data showed that:

- capital accumulation slowed in 20 countries;[4]

- the share of manufacturing in GDP in 18 countries stagnated or declined, an outcome to be expected in view of the almost universal slump in investment ratios. Therefore, the adjustment efforts of the 1980s seem to have led to, or not to have been able to prevent, shrinkage in an already underdeveloped industrial base;[5]

- export volumes declined in 13 of the 24 countries, while in the 11 countries in which export volumes increased, the impact on the balance of payments 'was almost always negligible.'[6]

It is not without reason, then, that Oxford's specialist in structural adjustment, Frances Stewart, has delivered the following judgement on the adjustment experience in Africa – a judgment that some would argue is understated:

The stabilization and adjustment policies advocated by the IMF and the World Bank and widely adopted in Africa have not succeeded in restoring growth in most countries; indeed, they have often been accompanied by continued economic deterioration. Moreover, in many respects, the policies are pushing African economies away from a desirable long-term structure especially because they are dampening comparative advantage in non-traditional agriculture and industry.[7]

Explaining Stagnation: 'Macro-Shocks' or Structural Distortions?

Why such a dismal record?

The problem, according to Massachusetts Institute of Technology (MIT) economist Lance Taylor and his associates, is that the World Bank and the IMF misdiagnosed the problem. The barrier to growth was not principally the 'distorted' economic structures of Third World economies but the two macroeconomic 'shocks' of the mid-1970s and early 1980s – the OPEC oil price rise and the debt crisis.[8] Indeed, using the Bank's own data, they suggest that the much-derided, market-distorting 'import-substitution strategy' that prevailed in Latin America during the period 1960–73 'was not that bad at fostering productivity.'[9] What mainly distinguished this earlier period from the 1980s was the massive external instability in the latter period, which led not only to a cutoff in capital inflows (except new money designated for repaying old debts) but also to a massive net outflow of resources that could otherwise have gone to domestic investment and sustained growth.[10] By ignoring the decisive importance of external conditions, the authors caution,

> there is a risk that IMF-inspired adjustment policies will drive their recipients toward prolonged 'stabilized stagnation' because these policies ignore crucial macroeconomic factors such as linked foreign exchange and fiscal constraints, financial fragility, and the dynamics of the inflation process.[11]

The Southeast Asian Case

The crucial role in growth played by external and macroeconomic stability is underlined by a comparison between Latin America and Southeast Asia. Unlike Latin America, Southeast Asia – with the exception of the Philippines – was not cut off from capital inflows in the 1980s. The case was quite the opposite, for there was a massive infusion of foreign capital in the form of Japanese investment in search of low-wage production sites after the yen's massive appreciation in 1985. Some $US15 billion worth of Japanese investment rushed into the region between 1985 and 1990,[12] and this made a critical contribution to inducing high or moderate growth rates in Singapore, Thailand, Indonesia, and Malaysia.

Malaysia is one of the few Third World countries that escaped stabilization or structural adjustment by either the World Bank or the IMF in the 1980s. In fact, it continued to maintain a protectionist trade regime, practised state-guided industrial targetting in key sectors such as the car industry and imposed strong controls on the operations of foreign investors. But Malaysia is now experiencing a 10 per cent growth rate, a development which is largely a result of the inflow of Japanese capital during the 1980s. Some US$2.2 billion flowed in between 1985 and 1990, or over $100 per citizen of Malaysia.

World Bank officials sometimes credit structural adjustment for Indonesia's growth rate of 5–6 per cent in the years 1985–1990. What they do not say is that economic liberalization has been quite limited, with the economy continuing to be marked by a high degree of protectionism, control by monopolies, and strong restrictions on foreign investment. What they do not acknowledge is the reality that

Indonesia's growth rate is more strongly correlated with the infusion of close to US$4 billion in Japanese investment during the same period. But Japan did not only bring in massive direct investments. When Indonesia's external accounts began to look shaky in the early eighties, Japan responded by devising a generous lending policy, which came to be known as a 'special credit', for a country that was regarded as a strategic source of raw materials.[13]

Thailand provides equally solid support for the thesis of Taylor and his associates that external stability rather than domestic 'distortions' was the principal barrier to economic growth in the 1980s. This country was subjected to structural adjustment in the early part of that decade, but it failed to put in place the World Bank's principal demand: the dismantling of the protectionist trade structure. Thailand did gear much of its manufacturing sector to export, but, like Indonesia and Malaysia, it did not accomplish this by opening up its domestic market, as prescribed by the Bank and Fund. Indeed, trade policies became even more protectionist and oriented toward import substitution during the second half of the 1980s, when Thailand's growth rate soared to double-digit levels.[14] It was not structural adjustment but the massive inflow of foreign investment, owing to the Japanese choosing Thailand as the fulcrum of their Southeast Asian operations that was central to sparking off the 8–10 per cent annual growth rates that dazzled the world in the late 1980s. Actually the protectionist 'distortions' probably facilitated growth, since a major reason for the Japanese car manufacturers' making major investments in Thailand was the desire to exploit that country's protected market. Unlike World Bank economists, Thai technocrats, in fact, have no qualms about acknowledging the source of their country's economic growth:

> The current explanation of Thailand's accelerated growth was the 1985 appreciation of the value of the yen, rendering Japanese production more costly. Japanese multinational companies were forced to look for new lower cost production locations. In 1987, Japanese investment approvals by Thailand's Board of Investments exceeded the cumulative Japanese investment for the preceding 20 years.[15]

Prescription for Stagnation

Taylor and his co-authors, in common with other academic critics of structural adjustment programs, have also stressed the way in which the different elements of the SAP set off, in the real world, a concatenation of events that brings about results that are different from those expected in IMF and World Bank theory. The different moments of this downward spiral could unfold as follows:

- Typically SAPs begin with stabilization measures such as tightening the money supply, letting interest rates rise, reducing government spending, and cutting wages. Inevitably, this forces a contraction of the economy.
- When devaluation is added to this policy of monetary and fiscal austerity to promote exports and earn foreign exchange, it escalates the contractionary effects by raising the local cost of imported capital and intermediate goods, leading to the 'policy "over-kill" for which the IMF is (un)justly famous.'[16]
- Economic contraction discourages private investors and left, to itself, the market does not automatically provide the signals that would renew private investor confidence in a declining economy.
- Nor does liberalization necessarily spark investment and growth in the agricultural sector, since the simplistic focus on lifting price controls on commodities fails to address the deeper structural, infrastructural, and technological barriers to production that are usually addressed by state-supported programs – which are, however, in the process of being dismantled in the name of fiscal discipline. For instance, letting the market determine fertilizer prices has led, in many African countries, to reduced applications, lower yields, and lower investment because of the absence of state-supported credit systems.[17]
- Where liberalization does lead to a rise in production, rising export income can trigger higher investment. But after an initial rise as producers respond to the SAP's export incentives, export income falls as world prices of the country's export commodities fall, precisely in response to the rising supply of the commodities stimulated by SAP programs in countries specializing in the same commodities. Besides, the lion's share of this falling income is allocated not to investment, but to debt servicing.
- This leaves 'public capital formation [as] the only vehicle for stimulating investment after adverse shocks.'[18] But, with its expenditures being slashed and its enterprises being shut down in order to reduce its role in economic life, the state cannot step in to reverse the decline in private investment.
- The end result of such macroeconomic management, says MIT economist Rudiger Dornbusch, is that the economy 'falls into a hole,'[19] or becomes stuck in a low-level trap, in which low investment, increased unemployment, reduced social spending, reduced consumption, and low output interact to create a vicious

cycle of stagnation and decline, rather than a virtuous circle of growth, rising employment, and rising investment, as originally envisaged by World Bank theory.[20]

The sharp disparity between the expected results of structural adjustment programs and their actual results is revealed by a brief survey of the dynamics of SAPs in three countries which have been promoted as success stories by the World Bank: Mexico, Chile, and Ghana.

Mexico: Model Reformer?

Mexico is often touted as being in the vanguard of structural reform in Latin America, owing to the commitment of its president, Carlos Salinas de Gortari, to the World Bank–IMF objective of opening up the local economy. Thus the country has received special attention from the Bretton Woods institutions, which have not passed up the slightest opportunity to proclaim the country a model debtor and exemplary reformer. An assessment of the actual impact of adjustment, however, renders questionable the contention that Mexico is a role model for the Third World.

First of all, Mexico has not derived significant debt relief, which was its principal aim in agreeing to undergo stabilization and structural adjustment programs at the hands of the World Bank and the IMF. A close look at the 1989 debt reduction agreement between Mexico, the private banks, and the World Bank and IMF underlines this. Trumpeted by the Bush administration as the model of the 'Brady Plan,' Washington's new policy to manage Third World debt, the Mexican agreement was said to reduce Mexico's debt to the banks by US$7 billion. But, as one debt expert points out, the net result was hardly any reduction, since Mexico had to borrow another US$7 billion to collateralize the deal fully – with US$5.8 billion of this new debt coming from the World Bank, the IMF, and other official sources.[21] What Mexico ended up with was not debt reduction but the usual debt rescheduling, in which maturities were stretched out over 30 years. That the Brady Plan did not bring genuine debt relief became even clearer later: in 1991 Mexico's debt was US$98 billion, or about $3 billion more than it had been when the agreement was concluded in 1989. And as a percentage of GDP, total external debt dipped only slightly, from 53 per cent in 1989 to 48 per cent in 1991.

In exchange for hardly any debt relief, Mexico ended up with even more onerous terms of structural adjustment from the World Bank, a set of conditions that former World Bank executive director Morris

In Tijuana, Mexico, refuse collectors wait to cross the highway to continue on to a dump site. Since the beginning of structural adjustment, poverty and inequality in Mexico have increased sharply. (Photo: Robert Gumpert)

Miller described as 'an unprecedented thorough-going interventionism ... to implement a program calling for the reduction of import barriers and export subsidies and other measures which indicate "a commitment to market-oriented economic reforms".'[22]

This intensified structural adjustment of 1989 followed six years of already close surveillance of Mexico by the IMF and the Bank, following the eruption of the debt crisis in 1982. The ultimate aim of these seven years' adjustment was supposed to be sustained growth achieved through the elimination of 'distortions' in the economy. The theory was that efficient production would be promoted by a reduced government role in the economy and demand-management policies including wage restraint, devaluation of the currency, and liberalization of foreign trade. The reality was that the private banks' claims on Mexico's financial resources and the World Bank and IMF's draconian efforts to 'restore macroeconomic equilibrium' and remake Mexico into a 'market-friendly' economy choked off domestic investment.

Capital expenditures as a percentage of total government expenditures dropped from 19.3 per cent in 1982 to 4.4 per cent in 1988, while interest payments on the country's domestic and foreign debt rose from 19 to 57 per cent of total government expenditures during the same period.

With very limited access to world capital markets, owing to its status as a 'problem debtor', and with limited sources of domestic financing, the bulk of Mexico's debt service payments could only be derived from foreign exchange gained by its exports. To promote greater export competitiveness, the authorities complied with the World Bank–IMF demand to undertake a series of devaluations of the peso relative to the dollar. But increased exports from Mexico actually contributed to lowering their price in world markets, so that the value of Mexico's exports was actually less in 1988 than it had been 1982. Thus, as a percentage of Mexico's exports of goods and services, debt service payments averaged a high 55 per cent between 1982 and 1988.

With so much financial resources – some 7–11 per cent of GDP each year – leaving the country in debt service, it was not surprising that little was left for investment by government, which was anyway being eased out of its role in production by structural adjustment policies. Without public investment to synergize it and discouraged by the squeeze in domestic demand imposed by wage cuts decreed by the IMF and World Bank, the private sector not only failed to invest, it left the country: by the beginning of the 1990s, Mexican citizens had 'well over $50 billion and perhaps even $100 billion, if one allows for accumulated interest' in assets abroad.[23] Not surprisingly, gross domestic investment declined by 1.9 per cent per annum in the 1980s.

Not surprisingly, too, Mexico's GDP saw no growth between 1982 and 1988, compared to an annual growth rate of 7 per cent in the 1970s. Since the country's population was increasing by about 2.3 per cent per year during this period, this meant that per capita GDP in 1988 had fallen back to its level of the late 1970s.

Trade liberalization contributed not only to the contractionary spiral but to deindustrialization. As import tariffs were lowered from 50 per cent to 20 per cent and import licenses were eliminated, bankruptcies cut a huge swathe across Mexico's industrial sector. With the closing down of hundreds of factories, the domestic textile and clothing sector shrunk radically – by 5 per cent in 1992 alone.[24]

Economic reversal of this magnitude could only have drastic social consequences. Debt expert Rudiger Dornbusch and investment banker Steven Marcus noted the 'frightening cost in real wage cuts,'[25] – cuts which amounted to over 41 per cent between 1982 and 1988. Depression of wages reduced labor's share of the national income from 43 per cent in 1980 to 35 per cent in 1987.[26] The unemployed rose to 20 per cent of the workforce and the under-employed to around 40 per cent.[27] These conditions drove half the population below the poverty line and worsened an already very unequal distribution of income.[28] The country was trapped in a vicious cycle of low consumption, low investment, and low output.

Despite the absence of genuine economic growth and the bleak social landscape created by structural adjustment, the Mexican government deepened its structural adjustment program into the 1990s. The privatization program was accelerated, with the result that the number of state enterprises was whittled down from 1,155 in 1982 to 285 by 1990.[29] Nine of 18 commercial banks taken over by the state during the debt crisis – so that the government could assume their obligations to foreign banks – were returned to private hands.[30] However, these moves did not produce free-market conditions but an economy dominated by a select few private interests, where 47 per cent of the GNP was controlled by 25 holding companies.[31]

Denationalization was also accelerated. The Salinas government liberalized the restrictive 1973 foreign investment code in 1989, loosening rules for foreign investor participation in areas such as the manufacture of automotive parts and telecommunications services and allowing 100 per cent foreign ownership in areas like private education, newspaper publication, and financial services.[32] Encouraged by these moves as well as by the prospect of Mexico becoming part of the North American Free Trade Agreement (NAFTA), a continent-wide market with few internal barriers, foreign investment flowed into Mexico, rising from US$2.6 billion in 1990 to $4.7 billion in 1991.[33] Among the key transactions with groups involving foreign investors were Anheuser-Busch's acquisition of a stake in the country's largest brewery and the sale of TELMEX (the country's second largest telephone company) and of the Companía Mexicana de Aviacion (the largest state-owned airline).[34]

But the dazzling inflow of foreign investment could not hide the reality that the economy has been severely weakened by structural adjustment. Despite the massive inflow of foreign investment, the GDP growth rate, which increased from 3.3 per cent in 1989 to 4.4 per cent in 1990, dropped to 2.7 per cent in 1992. Moreover, reflecting the shattering impact of adjustment on the country's industrial structure, this modest growth pushed the current account deficit from US$4 billion in 1989 to $20 billion in 1992, as demand sucked in imports of consumer, intermediate, and capital goods, a large part of which had formerly been filled by local products turned out by factories that were killed off by the SAP.

Mexican President Carlos Salinas de Gortari chides striking miners protesting his liberalization policies which have provoked widespread popular opposition. (Photo: Donna DeCesare, Impact Visuals)

By cutting domestic investment for years and radically reducing protection for local manufacturers, structural adjustment had made Mexico incapable of sustained growth without destabilizing its external accounts through massive imports. Thus, as Ricardo Grinspun and Maxwell Cameron note, the 'possibility that Mexico could face another loss of faith by foreign investors, another round of capital flight, and a large devaluation that would discredit the government is currently a matter for nervous speculation.'[35]

Chile as an Economic Laboratory

Chile is probably the country with the longest running structural adjustment program in the world, one which began with General Augusto Pinochet's 1973 bloody coup against the democratically elected government of President Salvador Allende. Adjustment took a particularly radical form, as Chilean economists trained at the University of Chicago sought to transform, via dictatorial power, an economy marked by heavy state intervention into an earthly version of the free-market paradise sketched out by Adam Smith in *The Wealth of Nations*. Not only were all the standard paraphernalia of structural adjustment programs called into play, but free-market pricing, trade and financial liberalization, monetary devaluation, export-oriented manufacturing, privatization, deregulation, and destatization were applied with an ideological vengeance.

By the end of the 1980s, Chile's economy had indeed been transformed:

- some 600 state enterprises had been sold off, with fewer than 50 remaining in private hands;[36]
- Chile had gone from being one of the most to one of the least protected Latin American economies, with all quantitative restrictions on trade abolished and tariffs set at a single flat rate of 10 per cent for all items;
- foreign investors had a strong presence in the economy, as part-owners of former state enterprises in such strategic sectors as steel, telecommunications, and airlines;
- radical deregulation of the domestic financial market had been accomplished;
- the economy had become substantially more integrated into the international economy, with total trade amounting to 57.4 per cent of GDP in 1990, compared to 35 per cent in 1970.[37]

Having supervised several stabilization and structural adjustment programs, the World Bank and the IMF had been central to this transformation, and they were proud of the results. However, many others raised the question: was it transformation or deformation?

Former dictator of Chile, General Augusto Pinochet, imposed repression as a necessary element of Chile's free-market experience. (Photo: Marcelo Montecino)

If success is to be measured by the stabilization of Chile's external accounts, then structural adjustment has had dubious results: Chile's external debt of US$19 billion in 1991 was higher than it had been at the start of the debt crisis in 1982; total debt stood at 49 per cent of GNP in 1991; and at that time close to 9 per cent of GDP was flowing out of the country to service the debt. This was, in fact, an understatement of debt-related outflow from the nation, since a significant portion of the debt had been transformed into foreign equity holdings in strategic sectors of the Chilean economy via debt–equity swaps.

If sustained growth is regarded as the key measure of the success of structural adjustment, then the results could hardly qualify as a success. As Ricardo Ffrench-Davis and Oscar Munoz point out, the growth in GDP during the Pinochet years (1974–89) averaged only 2.6 per cent a year, below the rates registered in the state-interventionist decades: 4 per cent in 1950–61 and 4.6 per cent in 1961–71.[38] The results of adjustment were more dismal when viewed in terms of growth in per capita GDP: this averaged 1.1 per cent in the 1970s and 0.9 per cent in the 1980s.[39]

The results are indeed meager when one considers that in order to obtain them, free-market policies plunged Chile into major depressions *twice* in one decade – first in 1974–5, when GDP fell by 12 per cent, then again in 1982–3, when it dropped by 15 per cent. One description of the Chilean experience that is more accurate than the orthodox account is provided by Lance Taylor and his associates, who write that 'the economy reeled through a 12-year sequence of disastrous stabilization experiments amply supported by the Bank and the Fund.'[40]

This wrenching restructuring of the Chilean economy was negative in more ways than one. The combination of a lower rate of investment and draconian trade liberalization resulted in deindustrialization: the manufacturing sector lost ground, declining from an average of 26 per cent of GDP in the late 1960s to an average of 20 per cent in the late 1980s. Indeed, from 1979 to 1981 manufacturing shrank in absolute terms, and it was not until 1988 that industrial value-added surpassed the absolute level attained in 1974.[41] As John Sheahan notes, 'The Chilean economy in the market-oriented liberalization phase … seemed to be moving toward de-industrialization in the name of efficiency and avoiding inflation.'[42]

Many metalworking and related manufacturing industries went under, while industries that were actually either resource-extracting or resource-processing activities – such as forestry, fishing, fruit-growing, and mining – were the ones that thrived in a political economy which favored exporting.[43] In structural terms, then, the Chilean economy, with its extreme dependence on exports of primary or processed goods and its shrinking manufacturing base, was likely to be more fragile by the late 1980s than it had been before the Pinochet period. ·

However, it is when one considers the social impact of radical free-market policy that the cost–benefit equation of structural adjustment lurches sharply towards the negative.

Despite their 'free-market' credentials, the Chilean economic authorities socialized the costs of adjustment in favor of the rich. The losses of close to US$3.5 billion – or nearly 20 per cent of GDP – in non-guaranteed foreign debt that were incurred by private institutions were absorbed by the government when Chile's debt crisis broke in 1983. Moreover, the Central Bank did not just prevent technically bankrupt banks from going under by providing large subsidies which amounted to about 4 per cent of GDP; it also kept in place their owners and managers.[44]

While it socialized the losses of the rich, the authorities dumped the burden of adjustment on to the poor and the middle class via a radical cutback in public spending, a tough freeze on wages, and a steep devaluation of the peso. The 24 per cent contraction of domestic expenditure provoked a 15 per cent drop in GDP and triggered unemployment, which rose to embrace over 30 per cent of the workforce in one year and remained at over 25 per cent for three years. And the 50 per cent real devaluation of the peso was translated mainly into a reduction of real wages by close to 20 per cent.[45]

While the rich debtors who were rendered technically bankrupt by the debt crisis received handsome subsidies, more than 50 per cent of the unemployed received no subsidy and the rest obtained only minor benefits.[46]

Thus, by the end of the decade both poverty and inequality had increased. The proportion of families living below the 'line of destitution' rose from 12 to 15 per cent between 1980 and 1990, and the percentage living below the poverty line (but above the line of destitution) rose from 24 to 26 per cent. This meant that at the end of the Pinochet period some 40 per cent, or 5.2 million, of a population of 13 million people were defined as poor in a country that had once boasted of having a large middle class. Poverty translated into hunger and malnutrition; for 40 per cent of the population the daily calorie intake dropped to 1,629 in 1990, from 2,019 in 1970 and 1,751 in 1980.[47]

In terms of income distribution, the share of the national income going to the poorest 20 per cent of the population fell from 4.6 per cent in 1980 to 4.2 per cent in 1990; over the same period the share going to the poorest 50 per cent declined from 20.4 per cent to 16.8 per cent; while the share going to the richest 10 per cent rose from 36.5 per cent to 46.8 per cent.[48]

To all these costs must be added the destruction of democracy that the Chilean 'Chicago Boys' felt was necessary to translate Milton Friedman's theories into reality.

In brief, through government intervention in a free-market experiment, the Chilean upper class had substantially increased its economic dominance. It is therefore understandable that a study for the Organization for European Cooperation and Development (OECD) asserted that the costs of the Chilean adjustment were 'among the largest in Latin America,' and concluded by posing the question: 'Would this type of adjustment have been feasible in a democratic regime?'[49]

Ghana: Beacon for Africa?

While structural adjustment has been personified in Mexico by Harvard-educated President Salinas and in Chile by the stern General Pinochet, in Ghana it is identified with Flight Lieutenant Jerry Rawlings, described by the London *Financial Times* as 'an enigma –

a firebrand socialist who has pursued one of the continent's most widely praised free-market economic reform programs, backed by aid from the World Bank and the International Monetary Fund.'[50]

Rawlings' Ghana is one of Africa's most 'structurally adjusted' economies, having concluded 16 stabilization and structural adjustment programs with the World Bank and the IMF since 1983.[51] The typical establishment view of the results of this diet of austerity, liberalization, devaluation, and destatization is contained in the same *Financial Times* article:

> These policies have given Ghana an average real growth rate of 5 per cent a year, reduced inflation from an annual rate of 123 per cent in 1983 to 18 per cent last year, restored confidence and stimulated investment and the return of millions of dollars held overseas by Ghanaian nationals. Debt arrears of $600 million were erased by 1990.[52]

This is, however, putting the best face on what is at best an ambiguous picture. Judged in terms of bringing about real debt relief, the Ghanaian structural adjustment program has so far been a failure: Ghana's external debt rose from US$1.7 billion at the beginning of structural adjustment in 1983 to $3.5 billion in 1990. As a percentage of GNP, external debt rose to 57 per cent in 1990 from 41 per cent in 1983; as a proportion of Ghana's exports of goods and services, it was slightly up from an astounding 345 per cent in 1983 to 353 per cent in 1990; and, as a percentage of exports of goods and services, debt service rose to 35 per cent in 1990, from 31 per cent in 1983.[53]

A key focus of structural adjustment in Ghana was improvement of the country's external accounts by reducing imports and increasing exports, particularly that of the main export, cocoa, through deep devaluation of the currency. But the current account registered deepening deficits at the end of the 1980s, for ironically, the SAP's focus on increasing exports,

> especially since it has occurred [simultaneously] in a large number of producing countries has led to a fall in world prices and lower earnings because of the low price elasticities for some crops. For example, cocoa and coffee prices dropped in the 1980s following output increases.[54]

The enormous rise in Ghanaian cocoa production was accompanied by a 48 per cent decline in the world cocoa price between 1986 and 1989; and the terms of trade went against Ghana, dropping from 100 in 1987 to 75 in 1990.[55]

In terms of growth, while it is true that Ghana's economy did grow at some 5 per cent a year in the latter half of the 1980s, GDP per capita at the end of the decade was actually just at the level it had reached at the start of the decade. Moreover, structurally, the economy had become much weaker. Import liberalization resulted in the loss of hundreds of private sector jobs in the textile industry [56] and the 'gradual demise of medium-large-scale domestic non-foreign controlled manufacturing industry.'[57] The Ghanaian experience reflected a larger continent-wide trend: the 10 industries that were the fastest growing employers in the 1970s in Africa were also the 10 industries that were the fastest growing disemployers in the 1980s.[58] This trend led economists Peter Robinson and Somsak Tambunlertchai to warn that the long-term result of trade liberalization 'could well be to foreclose the possibility of significant industrialization' in Africa.[59]

The program's strong bias toward incentives for export crops, particularly cocoa, and its negative measures against local food production, such as the removal of price subsidies for fertilizers, have weakened the latter, promoted dependency on food imports, and threaten 'to increase the vulnerability of the entire economy to the vagaries of the cocoa market.'[60]

Evaluating the social impact of adjustment, an OECD report concludes that Ghana's structural adjustment 'entailed great costs.'[61] Among the most severely disrupted areas was the informal sector, since the adjustment had 'the effect of suddenly cutting commercial margins and, consequently the incomes of small vendors, who are usually women.'[62] Also negatively affected were some 50,000 workers who lost their jobs on account of the huge cuts in the civil service demanded by the World Bank and the IMF in order to cut the budget deficit.[63] According to one account, the retrenchment covered 15 per cent of the entire labor force. In fact, these workers suffered a double blow with the simultaneous cutting of the informal market by adjustment measures, since, as the OECD notes, 'prior to adjustment these people were already poorly paid and were obtaining the majority of their income from informal trading activities.'[64]

In the cities, it appears that the only people who escaped relatively unscathed were high-level bureaucrats who were able to keep their jobs and managed, through various means, including corruption, to avoid the erosion of their income. In the countryside, where 'cocoa was king,' the higher prices for producers that came with structural adjustment did result in higher incomes for most of the 2 million farmers who raise cocoa. However, this result must be qualified, for

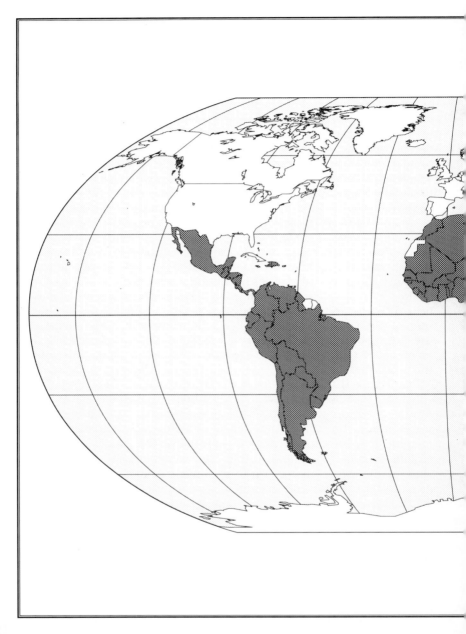

Global Reach: Map shows third world countries (shaded) which have undergone IMF and/or World Bank stabilization and structural adjustment programs in the period 1980–1991

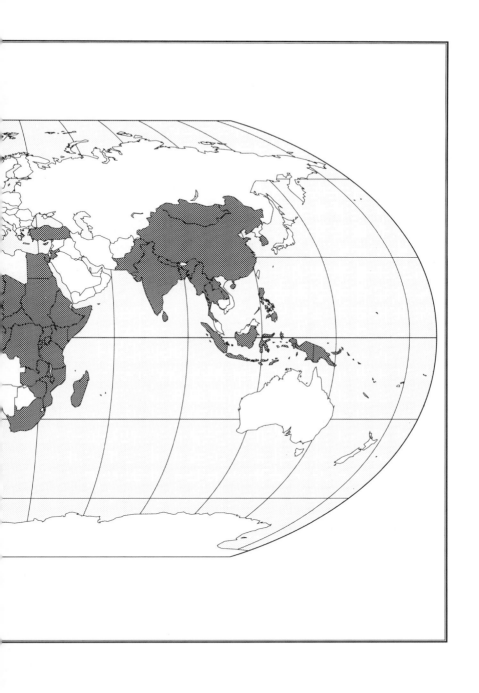

the increased income from cocoa was differentially appropriated by the different strata of cocoa producers. As the OECD notes:

> Cocoa is an important crop for the 'very poor,' the 'poor', and the 'rich' and so all these parts of the income distribution benefited from the reform. In proportionate terms, the 'rich' gained the most since the share of cocoa in total crop revenues is somewhat higher in the higher-income households.[65]

But higher prices for cocoa did not translate into higher incomes for all rural families. Indeed, non-cocoa food-crop producers saw their real incomes decline, owing to the removal of subsidies for fertilizers decreed by the structural adjustment program.[66]

To alleviate the suffering of the poor during the adjustment process, the World Bank and other international agencies devised the formidably named 'Programme of Actions to Mitigate the Social Costs of Adjustment' (PAMSCAD), which was designed to create a large number of public employment programs and help laid-off civil servants to find new jobs in agriculture. However, PAMSCAD's impact was limited. It was able to compensate for less than half the public sector jobs that had been eliminated by 1990.[67] Moreover, as Jeffrey Herbst points out, 'the PAMSCAD money that was supposed to go to the impoverished has been redirected to areas where the state already has a relatively strong administrative apparatus; that is, precisely the areas that have traditionally benefited from government programs.'[68]

Reviewing various surveys, Ghanaian economist Charles Abugre concludes that the available evidence suggests increasing inequality, declining food self-sufficiency, and rising absolute poverty.[69] Indeed, the higher incomes from cocoa exports have not substantially reduced the portion of the population living below the poverty line in the countryside, with the figure averaging 37 per cent in the 1980s.[70] As for the percentage of the urban population living below the poverty line, the only figure in Africa higher than Ghana's 59 per cent is that of famine-wracked Ethiopia.[71]

In sum, if one were to sum up the Ghanaian structural adjustment experience, one would have to point to a contradictory process marked by weak growth, accompanied by widening poverty and a structural weakening of the economy. This is hardly what one would call a success story.

6

Adjustment: the Costs

We did not think that the human costs of these programs could be so great, and the economic gains so slow in coming.

—World Bank Chief Economist for Africa, quoted in Morris Miller, *Debt and the Environment: Converging Crises* (New York: United Nations, 1991), p. 70)

[A]djustment is better for the poor than non-adjustment.

—World Bank, *Third Report on Adjustment Lending: Private and Public Resources for Growth,* Washington, DC, 1992

The rollback in income and living standards that hit the people of Mexico, Chile, and Ghana in the 1980s was part of a larger wave that overwhelmed much of the South during that decade. As it entered the 1990s, the South's grim condition was summed up by James Gustave Speth, president of the World Resources Institute:

The South is in crisis. In the developing countries, an estimated 13–18 million people, mostly children, die from hunger and poverty each year. That is about 40,000 people a day, or 1,700 people an hour ... Only 10–15 per cent of hunger stems from emergencies; most hunger – 85–90 per cent – is born of poverty.[1]

Though poverty and inequality were certainly widespread in the Third World before the 1980s, the evidence shows that they escalated sharply during that decade. While the adjustment policies of the Fund and the Bank were not the only cause of deepening poverty and growing inequality, they were a central link in a vicious circle whose other key elements were the cutting off of credit flows brought on by the debt crisis, increasing marginalization from flows of foreign direct investment, and deteriorating terms of trade owing to the sharply falling international price of the Third World's primary commodity exports and the inexorably rising price of its manufactured imports.

Misery: a Global Survey

Apart from East Asia and some areas in South Asia, most parts of the South experienced stagnation or sharp reversals in growth, escalating poverty, and increasing inequality both within and between countries.

With per capita income stagnant in the South and rising by 2.4 per cent a year in the North during the 1980s, the gap between living standards in North and South widened, with the average income in the North reaching US$12,510, or 10 times the average in the South, which was $710.[2] 'The global distribution of income still has the power to shock,' notes the United Nations Development Program; '77 per cent of the world's people earn 15 per cent of its income.'[3]

Especially ravaged during the decade were the regions that were most severely subjected to structural adjustment: Latin America and Africa. In Latin America, the force of adjustment programs struck with special fury, 'largely cancelling out the progress of the 1960s and 1970s.'[4] The numbers of people living in poverty rose from 130 million in 1980 to 180 million at the beginning of the 1990s.[5] (See Appendix 2 for rates of poverty and indigence in selected Latin American countries.) In a decade of negative growth, income inequalities – already among the worst in the world – worsened. As Enrique Iglesias, president of the Inter-American Development Bank (IDB), reports, 'the bulk of the costs of adjustment fell disproportionately on the middle and low-income groups, while the top five per cent of the population retained or, in some cases, even increased its standard of living.'[6] The top 20 per cent of the continent's population today earn 20 times that earned by the poorest 20 per cent.[7] In Brazil, a major victim of the debt crisis and a major target of adjustment, the top fifth earn 26 times more than the bottom fifth.[8]

With hunger and malnutrition on the rise, tuberculosis and cholera – diseases that had been thought to be banished by modern medicine – have returned with a vengeance throughout the continent, with cholera claiming at least 1300 in Peru alone in 1991.[9]

Among the more tragic consequences of widespread economic distress has been the wearing down of the social fabric. The renewed bout of *la violencia* in Colombia, for instance, cannot be divorced from the fact that during the late 1980s the country was transferring some 10 per cent of its GNP to its foreign creditors in the form of debt service. One can understand the attractions of the drug trade if one considers that, owing to harsh adjustment policies, per capita income in Colombia has been stagnant since the early 1980s. The poorest 40 per cent of households now have only 12.7 per cent of the national income, while unemployment in the poorest neighborhood of Medellin, from which most gangs emerge, is as high as 50 per cent.[10]

São Paulo, Brazil, 1984. As Brazil lurched deeper into economic crisis, popular protests and riots were not uncommon. (AP/Wide World Photos)

Similarly, the rising levels of violence in Peru, where the government and Shining Path guerrillas are engaged in bloody combat, cannot be divorced from the drastic social impact of disastrous depressive adjustment policies imposed by the IMF in the early 1980s. These measures claims Richard Webb, former president of Peru's Central Bank, pushed the economy into 'a series of vicious circles in which further adjustment efforts had both positive and negative effects, exacting a high price in both inflation and recession, and in political erosion, for marginal fiscal and balance-of-payments improvements.'[11]

But perhaps no event better exemplifies the link between adjustment policies and rising lawlessness than one which occurred in Brazil, the South's biggest debtor:

In 1991, the kidnappers of Francisco Jose Coeho Vieira, a Brazilian businessman, demanded a ransom of thirty-two thousand dollars – in food. When twenty tons of meat, sugar, pasta, beans, rice and milk were left near a Rio shantytown, a line of slum dwellers half a mile long battled for the goods. After fifteen minutes, everything was gone; five people were injured in the melee.[12]

Caracas, Venezuela, 1989. A policeman shoots into a crowd of people protesting hikes in transport fares. These measures were taken in response to IMF demands for cuts in the government's social spending. (AP/Wide World Photos)

Sub-Saharan Africa has been even more devastated than Latin America. So massive is the region's reversal of fortune that MIT's Lester Thurow has commented, with cynical humor tinged with racism: 'If God gave it [Africa] to you and made you its economic dictator, the only smart move would be to give it back to him.'[13]

Total debt for sub-Saharan Africa now amounts to 110 per cent of GNP, compared to 35 per cent for all developing countries.[14] Cut off from significant capital flows except aid, battered by plunging commodity prices, wracked by famine and civil war, and squeezed by structural adjustment programs, Africa's per capita income declined by 2.2 per cent per annum in the 1980s. By the end of the decade it had plunged to its level at the time of independence in the early 1960s. Some 200 million of the region's 690 million people are now classified as poor, and even the least pessimistic projection of the World Bank sees the number of poor rising by 50 per cent to reach 300 million by the year 2000.[15] If current trends continue, the United Nations Development Program estimates that the continent's share of the world's poor, now 30 per cent, will rise to 40 per cent by the year 2000.[16]

Impoverishment raised the incidence of undernutrition in the region from 22 per cent in the 1979–81 period to 26 per cent in 1983–85.[17] One study found that in Zambia adjustment reduced food consumption, with some families reducing the number of meals per day from an average of two to one.[18] As Eva Jespersen points out, women have been especially hard hit, since the higher physical demands on them, relative to men, necessitate calorie requirements that are often not met, especially for women engaged in producing cash crops. This deficiency could lead to 'low birthweight babies and a subsequent higher risk of infant morbidity and mortality.'[19]

Public health-care systems throughout the continent are 'collapsing from lack of medicines,'[20] according to a United Nations advisory group, and Africans are increasingly forced either to do without medical care or to obtain it from essentially private systems. In Zaïre, this trend toward privatization has forced 'women with few skills [to] resort to petty trade, food preparation, illegal beer and alcohol production, market gardening, sewing, smuggling, and prostitution.'[21]

With radical retrenchment of public health-care, owing to World Bank- and IMF-imposed budget cuts, Africa is very vulnerable to resurgent cholera, which is now spreading at what the World Health Organization has characterized as a 'catastrophic pace,' owing to the breakdown of water and sewage systems triggered by the economic crisis.[22] And the continent lies practically defenseless against the AIDS epidemic, which now threatens to decimate the most productive stratum of the population – those aged between 20 and 45 years old. The statistics are chilling: surveys have found that in Zimbabwe some 50 per cent of the armed forces carry the AIDS virus;[23] in Kampala, Uganda, more than 25 per cent of women seen in maternity clinics are HIV-positive;[24] and in Zambia 20 to 25 per cent of various groups in the capital, Lusaka, are infected.[25]

Yet the resources which are badly needed to combat AIDS are going elsewhere, with a significant portion earmarked for debt servicing: 24 per cent of foreign exchange earnings in the case of Zimbabwe, 13 per cent in that of Zambia, and 71 per cent in Uganda.

So evident is the role of structural adjustment programs in the creation of this devastated landscape that the World Bank chief economist for Africa has admitted: 'We did not think that the human costs of these programs could be so great, and the economic gains so slow in coming.'[26]

Questionable Evidence

Other World Bank officials have been less frank, countering that 'the available evidence on changes in income aspects of poverty ...

indicates that adjustment is better for the poor than non-adjustment.'[27] For proof, they point to only two countries, Costa Rica and Indonesia, and even here they provide few or confusing details to support their contention.[28]

The reduction of the percentage of Indonesia's population living below the poverty line from 60 per cent in 1970 to 17 per cent in 1987 is one of the great mysteries of our time, for the drop took place at a time when there was only moderate economic growth and little change in a very skewed distribution of income. Most likely, says one specialist in Southeast Asian poverty, the 'poverty reduction' is a statistical rather than a real phenomenon – the result of 'bad record-keeping by government statisticians, where the poverty line index just kept being shifted downwards and with no adjustments made for past data.'[29]

A similar problem hobbles the Bank's claim that in Costa Rica the incidence of poverty has declined from 25 per cent to 10 per cent, even when the annual GNP growth rate has been low and per capita income has stagnated. What would have made this claim credible is a phenomenon that was also absent in Indonesia: a significant change in income distribution. But in fact income distribution worsened during the 1980s, in a country which already had a income distribution structure similar to Chile's, with the top 20 per cent of all families accounting for 55 per cent of household income.[30] Given this trend in income distribution, the poverty data of the UN Economic Commission for Latin America, which show an increase in the number of households living in poverty from 22 to 24 per cent between 1980 and 1990, are more believable. (See Appendix 2.)

Adjusting the Environment

While some structural adjustment programs, such as those in Ghana, tried belatedly, though unsuccessfully, to address the social costs of adjustment, no structural adjustment program has explicitly been designed to take the environment into account. As a result, heightened environmental degradation and resource exploitation have often accompanied structural adjustment efforts.

Indeed, it is hard to see how structural adjustment can be made environment-friendly, since it usually contributes to impoverishment and more inequality, which are two of the key causes of environmental degradation. This is not to say that poor people harm the environment because they are poor. Many tribal and peasant communities have, in the past, developed ecologically benign systems of sustenance.

This equilibrium, however, has been disrupted in recent times by the dynamics of impoverishment triggered by the development of unequal control over land and resources, subjection of the economy to external forces, and rapid population growth. This mutually reinforcing relationship between impoverishment and ecological degradation is described by the 1992 *World Bank Development Report*:

> Because they lack resources and technology, land-hungry farmers resort to cultivating erosion-prone hillsides and moving into tropical forest areas where crop yields on cleared fields usually drop sharply after just a few years. Poor families often have to meet urgent short-term needs, prompting them to 'mine' natural capital through, for example, excessive cutting of trees for firewood and failure to replace soil nutrients.[31]

The Bank then uses Africa as an example of the vicious cycle of impoverishment and ecological disruption, overlooking the fact that, together with the IMF, it has been responsible for the policies that deepened the poverty of the continent in the 1980s:

> Agricultural stagnation in Sub-Saharan Africa is a particularly clear example of the mutually reinforcing nexus of poverty, population growth, and environmental damage. Low agricultural productivity, caused mainly by poor incentives and poor provision of services, has delayed the demographic transition [to lower birth rates] and encouraged land degradation and deforestation, which in turn lowered productivity. Africa's forest declined by 8 per cent in the 1980s; 80 per cent of Africa's pasture and range areas show signs of damage; and in such countries as Burundi, Kenya, Lesotho, Liberia, Mauritania, and Rwanda [all of which were under IMF and/or World Bank programs – author's note] fallow periods are often insufficient to restore soil fertility.[32]

The debt crisis and structural adjustment of the 1980s heightened the interaction between impoverishment and environmental degradation, as increasing poverty and the external debt drove poor people and poor countries to exploit lands and forests more intensively, either for subsistence or for export. For instance, most of the top 15 Third World debtors have tripled the rate of exploitation of their forests since the late 1970s, a phenomenon that is undoubtedly related to both the survival imperative of poor, landless people and the pressing need of nations to gain foreign exchange in order to make interest payments. Indonesia and Brazil, two heavily indebted countries that also happen to contain much of the planet's remaining forests, have seen their rates of deforestation increase by 82 per cent and 254 per cent respectively since the late 1970s.[33]

But beyond poverty and indebtedness was another factor driving more intensive resource exploitation. This was the ideological bias of the standard SAP against any disincentives that might stand in the way of the operation of market forces which were seen as the *élan vital* of growth and prosperity. This translated into opposition on the part of the economic authorities to effective environmental regulation by the state.

A close look at four countries – Chile, Costa Rica, Ghana, and the Philippines – reveals the dynamics of this vicious circle of poverty, structural adjustment, market ideology, and environmental degradation.

Intensified Resource Extraction in Chile
In Chile, ideological preferences, pressure to gain foreign exchange to make debt repayments, and the desire to attract foreign investment combined to prevent the government from imposing any meaningful environmental controls over the exploitation of natural resources on which Chile based its export drive during the 1980s.

Wood has been one of the mainstays of Chile's export offensive, with exports doubling between 1983 and 1989. Increasingly, timber production comes from industrial plantations, but in the rush to make plantations the cornerstone of Chile's forest products industry, much natural forest was cut down and replaced by pine monocultures.[34] As Sandra Postel and John Ryan note, 'When a cathedral grove of millenia-old *alerce* trees in Chile – containing some of the world's oldest living organisms – is cut, no statistics can capture the world's loss.'[35]

As for the fishing industry, the annual sardine catch in 1987 and 1988 was about 2.2 million and 1.5 million tons respectively, far above the 1 million ton limit to prevent over-exploitation.[36] It is therefore not surprising that the total fish catch declined by 16 per cent in 1989 and another 22 per cent in 1990.[37]

Overfishing was not, however, the only reason for the reduced catch. Other contributing factors were the runoffs from mining operations and pesticides which seeped into rivers and were then carried out to sea. *El Mercurio*, the conservative Chilean daily newspaper, notes that 'industrial wastes, primarily from the large mining companies, in the form of tailings or surpluses from the copper-refining process ... [have] seriously affected the coastal area of the Second and Third regions.'[38] The problem is not the lack of environmental laws. Rather, as one study notes, 'The Chilean government has been particularly loath to force state-owned mineral operations to comply with the laws. At times, the prospect of major revenue from projects leads government officials to simply ignore environmental rules or studies.'[39]

As for pesticides, not only were runoffs contributing to the reduced fish catch, but their heavy use threatened the health of producers and consumers alike. So heavy is the pesticide-dependence of Chilean fruit exports that Chilean grapes, which account for one-fourth of grapes consumed in the US, were temporarily banned from entering the United States in 1990.

The rape of Chile's environment that all these 'externalities' of unrestrained entrepreneurship added up to was noted in a government report cited by the *New York Times* which asserted that

> the economic growth of Chile has taken place at the expense of the environment ... [T]he so-called export 'boom' was based on the use and abuse of natural resources, permitting the degradation of the eco-systems greater than their ability to regenerate.[40]

Adjustment and Deforestation in Costa Rica

Costa Rica was subjected to 9 IMF and World Bank stabilization and structural adjustment programs between 1980 and 1989. As in Chile, a key aim of the adjustment was to make the Costa Rican economy more efficient by opening up the domestic economy to imports and foreign investment and by boosting the country's export industries in order to gain foreign exchange. Two key export industries, in particular, benefitted from adjustment policies: the banana industry and cattle raising. The accelerated development of these sectors, however, was achieved at a high environmental cost.

In the banana industry, expansion was encouraged by structural adjustment policies that not only produced deep tax cuts on banana exports but gave new banana producers generous subsidies 'to strengthen Costa Rica's international competitiveness.'[41] This windfall triggered the expansion of both foreign-owned and domestic plantations, which in turn accelerated what was already an advanced stage of deforestation. Perhaps the most cogent description of the environmental consequences of these export-driven policies is provided by one of their key supporters, the World Bank:

> Starting in 1986, plantations expanded again, at a rate of 2,000 ha per year. More important, regarding deforestation, however, is that the banana growing area has shifted almost completely from the South Pacific to the Atlantic Region ... It is estimated that production will expand in this region by 5,000 ha by 1993 at the

expense of forest cover. This expansion, accompanied by land invasion by plantation workers, is said to constitute a major threat to the protected areas of Tortuguero [on Costa Rica's northeast coastline]. From an environmental point of view, aside from the issues related to banana production (pesticides, solid waste pollution, sedimentation), the expansion of banana plantations gives rise to concern because it threatens the area's biodiversity.[42]

Deforestation was not the only form of environmental degradation triggered by the expansion of banana plantations. The industry is heavily dependent on pesticide use, leading, according to a study by the School of Environmental Sciences at Costa Rica's National University, to serious health problems for banana workers, including 'spells of vomiting, dizziness, headaches, eye lesions, skin burns, and allergies.'[43] Moreover, once deforested areas were planted with

US Standard Fruit Banana Plantation at Valle de Estrella, Costa Rica. Structural adjustment in Costa Rica benefitted plantation owners, while the laborers and their families fell deeper into poverty. (Photo: Donna DeCesare, Impact Visuals)

bananas, soil degradation accelerated, since bananas rapidly deplete soil of its humus and nitrogen. To sustain banana production, the banana companies substituted huge amounts of chemical fertilizers for natural nutrients. These fertilizers then mixed with pesticides to form chemical runoffs that washed into rivers and eventually into the sea. The destruction of some 90 per cent of the coral reef in Talamanca, a region on Costa Rica's southeastern coast, is linked to these chemical runoffs.[44]

Another key beneficiary of Costa Rica's SAP which has contributed to environmental damage is cattle raising, which services the international fast-food industry. To foster export expansion, a third of state-financed agricultural credit has gone to cattle ranchers. They have responded by turning forests into pasture land more rapidly. The proportion of the national territory under forest cover dropped from half in 1970 to 31 per cent in 1987,[45] and 70 per cent of deforested land is now used for pasture.[46] So intensely do ranchers covet forest land that in Costa Rica, 'ranchers practice 'fence-creeping' – literally edging their fences beyond their property lines into national parks.'[47] Yet tropical soils without forest cover quickly degrade, leading the ranchers to abandon the land within a decade and generating constant pressure to bring new forested land into pasture.[48]

SAP and Ghana's Environment

The focus of Ghana's structural adjustment program was to make cocoa production more profitable for farmers so that they could increase output, resulting in greater foreign exchange earnings for Ghana. Output rose, but, as pointed out earlier, precisely because of this, the price of cocoa fell on world markets because of finite demand. With the value of exports flat and imports inexorably rising, this led to a worsening of the current account balance from a deficit of US$43 million in 1986 to a deficit of $229 million in 1990.

To make up for the fragile state of the cocoa industry, the government moved to revive commercial forestry, with World Bank support. Timber production rose from 147,000 cubic meters to 413,300 cubic meters in the period 1984–7, accelerating the destruction of Ghana's already much-reduced forest cover. With deforestation proceeding at a rate of 1.3–2 per cent a year, Ghana's tropical forest is now just 25 per cent of its original size,[49] and the country, according to a study of the World Watch Institute, will soon make the transition from a net exporter to a net importer of wood.[50] Indeed, economist Fantu Cheru predicts that Ghana could well be stripped of trees by the year 2000.[51]

Deforestation has triggered a vicious ecological cycle, leading, according to Development GAP, to regional climatic change, soil erosion, and large-scale deforestation. Moreover, deforestation

also threatens household and national food security now and in the future. Seventy-five per cent of Ghanaians depend on wild game to supplement their diet. Stripping the forest has led to sharp increases in malnutrition and disease. For women, the food, fuel, and medicines that they harvest from the forest provide critical resources, especially in the face of decreased food production, lower wages, and other economic shocks that threaten household food security.[52]

Forest destruction, however, is but one of the many dimensions of environmental destruction wrought by structural adjustment. Charles Abugre calls attention to the fact that

the rapid mining of environmental resources as evidenced by fast depleting forests, bush-fires ravaged savanna lands as well as open-cast mining without land reclamation plans, deep sea over-fishing and the reckless dumping of toxics from mines and industries are undermining the main assets of the poor – land and water resources.[53]

Intensifying the Philippine Environmental Crisis

Like Ghana, the Philippines has been one of the most structurally adjusted countries, as it has been 'on the cure' almost continuously since 1980. Structural adjustment, in fact, has been one of the threads of continuity between the newly elected government of Fidel Ramos, the recent government of Cory Aquino, and the dictatorship of Ferdinand Marcos.

There appears to be a strong consensus that the stabilization programs of the IMF and the World Bank during the 1980s had a strong negative impact on the environment. A World Resources Institute locates the problem in the sharply escalating pressures on the country's fragile natural resource base that were brought about by the economic contraction triggered by the SAP. Adjustment

created so much unemployment that migration patterns changed drastically. The large migration flows to Manila [the capital] declined, and most migrants could turn only to open access forests, watersheds, and artisanal fisheries. Thus the major environmental

---

Structural adjustment in Ghana has led to a deteriorating infrastructure and increasing poverty. (Mark Edwards, Still Pictures)

Smokey Mountain, Manila, Philippines. Refuse pickers comb through the garbage looking for anything that can be reused or sold. This smoldering mountain of trash symbolized the Philippines economic crisis. (Robert Gumpert)

effect of the economic crisis was over-exploitation of these vulnerable resources.[54]

While exploitation of natural resources for subsistence needs increased during the 1980s, resource exploitation for commercial purposes, both for domestic consumption and export, declined. This was due to to a combination of an overexploited resource base and lower demand owing to global economic stagnation in the middle of the decade. Nonetheless, the IMF–World Bank pressure on the country to gain foreign exchange in order to service the external debt still resulted in a substantial outflow of natural resources, accounting for almost US$23 billion of the $50 billion worth of products exported by the Philippines between 1981 and 1989.[55] And it discouraged serious government efforts to impose environmental controls on resource use.

The staggering consequences of the vicious interaction of impoverishment, adjustment, export-orientation, and environmental degradation included the following:

- the portion of the country covered by forest declined from 34 per cent in the mid-1960s to 21 per cent in the mid-1980s;[56]
- coastal fish resources were depleted, as the annual fish catch rose to an average of 374,000 tons a year in 1980–4, from 311,000 in 1970–4;[57]
- 70 per cent of coral reefs, have been destroyed in the last 15 years alone,

> thanks to a combination of siltation from denuded mountains, tailings from mines, and harmful fishing techniques [including] gargantuan drift nets used by foreign fishing fleets, dynamite blasting by fisherfolk in search of quick and easy catches, and cyanide squirted into the reefs to stun and catch the exotic tropical fish about half of which will end up inhabiting aquariums in US homes...;[58]

- and of the Philippines' original 500,000 hectares of mangroves, the coastal breeding grounds of fish, only 38,000 hectares remain,[59] much of the rest having been converted into fish or prawn farms geared mainly to producing for foreign markets.

Prawn farming in the Philippines, in fact, provides a good illustration of the devastating environmental impact of debt-driven, export-oriented production. With World Bank encouragement, the Philippines went into prawn farming in a big way in the 1980s, with the value of prawn exports, most of whch are exported to Japan, growing eightfold between 1980 and 1987.[60] Intensive prawn farming necessitates a mix of fresh and salt water, which explains why prawn ponds are located on the coast: vast quantities of fresh water are pumped from underground aquifers and mixed with salt water from the ocean. However, as Robin Broad and John Cavanagh point out,

> the parched underground aquifer begins to suck in water from the sea, raising salinity levels. This inland water migration ... left unchecked ... will eventually ruin the land for agriculture – and, ironically, for aquaculture too. Experts claim that it would take a generation after the prawn farms stopped operating to flush out the salinity.[61]

By the end of the 1980s, the Philippines had indeed been reduced to a 'plundered paradise,' to borrow Broad and Cavanagh's description, and a not insignificant factor in this had been the seemingly endless adjustment process.

Former Philippine President Ferdinand Marcos, a World Bank favorite, supported structural adjustment programs while his country spiraled into environmental, social, and economic decline. (Photo: John M. Miller, Impact Visuals)

7

Adjustment: the Outcome

If God gave it [Africa] to you and made you its economic dictator, the only smart move would be to give it back to him.

—Lester Thurow, *Head to Head: the Coming Struggle among Japan, Europe, and the United States* (New York: William Morrow, 1992)

Not since the conquistadores plundered Latin America has the world experienced a [financial] flow in the direction we see today.

—Morris Miller, former executive director for Canada at the World Bank, *Debt and the Environment: Convergent Crises* (New York: United Nations, 1991)

Judged by its ostensible objectives of resolving the debt problems of Third World economies, sanitizing their external accounts, and bringing about renewed and sustained growth, structural adjustment has been, for the most part, a resounding failure.

But judged by its underlying strategic goals of shoring up the interest of the North and resurbordinating the South within a North-dominated international economic system, structural adjustment has undoubtedly been a tremendous success.

Ending the Creditors' Crisis

An immediate objective of the stabilization and adjustment programs was to rescue the Northern financial interests which had become over-exposed in the Third World. To accomplish this, the World Bank and the IMF became the lynchpin of a strategy that involved providing compliant Third World debtors with billions of dollars in quick-disbursing SAL or standby loans which would then be transferred as interest payments to the coffers of the private banks.

Reflecting this strategy, the flow of commercial bank credit to the Third World plummeted, while that of the official finance institutions increased sharply: in 1981, commercial banks supplied 42 per cent of net credit flows to the Third World and official finance institutions 37 per cent, but by 1988 the private banks provided only 6 per cent of net debt flows and official finance institutions 88 per cent of the total. Most of the inflow of official money was used by debtors to service their debt to the private banks. Between 1982 and 1986 Third World countries received US$25 billion more from official creditors than they paid out to them, while they paid the commercial banks $183 billion more in interest and amortization than they received in new bank loans.[1] Since the private banks' exposure in the Third World had been reduced only slightly, most of the inflow of official money went not to relieving the principal but to meeting current interest payments.

Essentially, this was using international public money to bail out the Northern banks. As one debt specialist describes it, 'lending banks were buying ... time at the expense of their governments. Banks were getting out from under by shifting more and more of the risk onto official lenders.'[2] This was, of course, not the only instance of the 'socialization' of the consequences of the foreign private banks' hothouse lending policies: as noted earlier, the governments of the indebted countries also assumed the obligation of repaying to foreign commercial banks the bad debts that had been incurred by local private institutions. In short, free-market ideology stopped at the water's edge.

Having saved the commercial banks from the threat of default at the hands of the debtors by lending the latter public money for interest payments, the Bank and the IMF then went on to apply the draconian adjustment policies which would assure a steady supply of repayments in the medium and long term. A focus on production for export combined with the repression of consumption via a wage freeze or rollback, and cutbacks in government expenditure, it was hoped, would produce foreign exchange that would not be derailed into buying imports but channelled into servicing the foreign debt. This policy was enormously successful, effecting as it did an astounding net transfer of financial resources from the Third World to the commercial banks that amounted to US$178 billion between 1984 and 1990.[3] So massive was the decapitalization of the South that a former director of the World Bank exclaimed, 'Not since the conquistadores plundered Latin America has the world experienced a flow in the direction we see today.'[4]

World Bank-IMF intervention saved the commercial banks from the threat of default and bought them time to build up loan-loss reserves both to insulate them against debt repudiation and, by the 1990s, to reduce their exposure in the Third World relative to their capital. By 1992, the tenth anniversary of the debt crisis, the exposure of US banks in the South had dropped from its 1987 level of 140 per cent of equity to 29 per cent. [5] For all intents and purposes, the crisis was over for the creditors.

It was a different story for the Third World debtor countries, who saw their total external debt climb to US$1.3 trillion in 1992, from $785 billion in 1982. Few countries were able to achieve a net reduction in their debt to the banks, having obtained concessions mainly along the lines of the rescheduling or stretching out of maturities, slight reductions in interest rates charged to their debt load, and securitization or the conversion of debt into low-interest bonds. For some countries, in fact, debt agreements entered into with the banks merely legitimized their arrears and formalized the low levels of repayment that they had actually been capable of making. It was estimated that arrears on interest payments in Latin America and the Caribbean had reached US$25 billion at the end of 1991.[6] (See Appendix 3 for external accounts of selected Third World countries.)

The main difference between the situation in 1982 and that in 1993 lay, as has already been alluded to, in the composition of the debt load: in 1993, a fairly big portion of the Third World debt was owed to official finance institutions such as the Bank and the Fund, which had loaned governments money to make interest payments to the private banks. Now those loans were falling due, and themselves becoming a source of stress. Indeed, in the late 1980s both the IMF and the International Bank for Reconstruction and Development (the non-concessional lending window of the World Bank) became net recipients of financial resources from sub-Saharan Africa. [7] But there was no intention at the Bank or the Fund of softening the terms of repayment.

Despite the chorus in Wall Street and London that the last rites are being administered to the debt crisis,[8] the South continues to be impaled on the horns of the dilemma described by Lester Thurow; 'Latin America cannot grow if they must service international debts as large as those that now exist. Too many resources have to be taken out to pay interest on those debts; too few are left for reinvestment.'[9] And with no end in sight to the debt crisis, many peoples in the South are becoming convinced that *that* – the imposition of a state of permanent stagnation – was precisely the idea.

The New South

What is of more consequence, however, than the rescue of the Northern commercial banks and the massive redistribution of financial resources from the South to the North was the achievement, by the end of the 12-year-long Reagan–Bush era in Washington, of the strategic objective of structural adjustment: the imposition of reforms that have since transformed scores of Third World economies. From Argentina to Ghana, state participation in the economy has been drastically curtailed; government enterprises are passing into private hands in the name of efficiency; protectionist barriers on Northern imports have been eliminated wholesale; restrictions on foreign investment have been lifted; and, through export-first policies, the internal economy has been more tightly integrated into the capitalist world market.

This common consequence of structural resubordination to the North via the dismantling of the economic role of the state has taken place under leaders as politically diverse as the Peronist Carlos Menem in Argentina, the social democrat Michael Manley in Jamaica, the socialist Jerry Rawlings in Ghana, the Nasserite Hosni Mubarak in Egypt, and the technocrat Carlos Salinas de Gortari in Mexico.

Most political figures have, in fact, been reduced to the role of legitimizing policies worked out between the Fund, the Bank, and foreign-educated technocrats. Since many of these technocrats came from the same schools which produced their Bank and Fund counterparts or were themselves former employees of these institutions, it is not surprising that they shared a common belief in the achievement of growth and efficiency via an expansion of the freedom of international capital and an extension of the reign of the market throughout the globe. It was the prior internalization of this ideology within a significant section of Third World elites that accounted for the universal adoption of the IMF-World Bank-prescribed structural adjustment programs when crisis overtook the Third World economies in the early 1980s. Perhaps the best representative of this governing elite and its technocratic internationalism was Mexico's Salinas, a holder of a Harvard economics doctorate, who defined his mission as the reversal of the nationalist and social gains of the Mexican Revolution in the name of efficiency and growth.

It is testimony to the potent combination of technocratic free-market ideology and Northern economic power that, despite the dismal record of failures in the 1980s, most Third World elites saw few alternatives to structural adjustment in the 1990s. Indeed, one of the prized targets of the Northern offensive fell in 1991: India, a leader of the Non-Aligned Movement and long a champion of state-led nationalist development, promised a thoroughgoing restructuring of its economy in exchange for a SAL that would assist it in servicing its debts to Western banks. Conservative circles ascribed almost as much significance to the event as to the concurrent dismantling of socialism in the Soviet Union.

The surrender of leading countries like India to structural adjustment translated in the global arena into a deep erosion of the power and prestige of those institutions that had served as agents of Southern interests: the Non–Aligned Movement, UNCTAD, the Group of 77. The decomposition of the Third World was felt at the United Nations, where the United States was emboldened once again to use that body to front Northern interests, including providing legitimacy for the US-led invasion of Iraq in 1991.

Rollback had succeeded.

And as the Third World entered what promised to be an even bleaker decade than the 1980s, the South Commission captured the essence of the contemporary condition of the South: [I]t may not be an exaggeration to suggest that the establishment of a system of international economic relations in which the South's second-class status would be institutionalized is an immediate danger.'[10]

8

Resubordinating the NICs

> Although the NICs may be regarded as tigers because they are strong, ferocious traders, the analogy has a darker side. Tigers live in the jungle, and by the law of the jungle. They are a shrinking population.
>
> —David Mulford, senior official, US Treasury Department, 'Remarks before the Asia-Pacific Capital Markets Conference,' San Francisco, November 17, 1987.

While structural adjustment has been the North's principal instrument in resubordinating the South, when it came to the NICs, or 'newly industrializing countries,' trade policy was its weapon of choice.

It might seem an exaggeration to describe the US as engaged in a crusade to 'adjust the NICs.' After all, were not the East Asian economies of Hong Kong, Singapore, Taiwan, and South Korea success stories of capitalism? Had not Ronald Reagan himself, in his 1985 State of the Union address, depicted the NICs as shining examples of the magic of the market?:

> America's economic success ... can be repeated a hundred times in a hundred nations. Many countries in East Asia and the Pacific have few resources than the enterprise of their own people. But through free markets they've soared ahead of centralized economies.[1]

From Allies to Targets

True, the NICs were deployed as ideological weapons in the Cold War. Yet even as they were extolled as free-market models, many US policymakers knew that their success was not a product of the unfettered operation of the laws of the market but stemmed mainly from the commanding role of the state in most of these economies. In fact, the economy of South Korea, the NIC par excellence, could perhaps be most accurately described as a 'command capitalist' regime, where the state built up industry not only by putting into place trade and investment regimes favoring domestic enterprises, but also by engaging in production itself, with singular success.[2]

72

This positive experience in state-managed production was exemplified by the Pohang Iron and Steel Company (POSCO), the establishment of which was opposed by the World Bank in the early 1970s. But by the mid-1980s POSCO had become one of the world's most efficient steelmakers; for each ton of steel it produced it employed half the number of workers that British Steel needed to produce the same amount.[3] More important, POSCO became central to Korea's transition from an exporter of labor-intensive commodities to an exporter of higher value-added, technology-intensive products, since it 'was able to provide related industries with a steady supply of steel products at low prices, thus sharpening Korea's competitive edge in such industries as shipbuilding, automobiles, construction, and electronics.'[4]

During the 1960s and 1970s, however, the distinctively statist policies of the NICs were overlooked by Washington's containment liberals and advocates of realpolitik in foreign policy, both of whom placed the overriding emphasis on a political alliance with these front-line states in the struggle with global communism. An additional incentive for looking the other way was the NICs' serving as cheap-labor havens for US corporations seeking to escape the high wages of US labor. Set up for the assembly of goods that were then reexported to the US, the TNC manufacturing operations in 'export-processing zones' were critical elements in the globalization of the transnationals' production process.

But by the early 1980s, US policy toward the NICs began to change. Triggering this transformation was the increasing prosperity of these state-led economies. This provoked the coming together of US industries threatened by NIC imports, resentful US corporations which felt excluded from growing NIC domestic markets because of import and investment restrictions, angry high-tech companies seeking to end NIC 'pirating' of their technology, and US agricultural interests seeking expanded access to these markets to dump their surpluses. 'Free Trade' became the rallying cry for these interests, and this slogan struck a resonant chord among ideological free marketeers who accompanied Ronald Reagan to Washington.

Thus, while the Reagan administration continued to extoll Korea as a front-line political ally, it began to evolve a tough economic policy toward that country. Although the immediate goal of the evolving policy was to eliminate the US trade deficit with the NICs, its strategic purpose was to reduce the threat they posed to US economic interests by rolling back the state from its leading role in the high-speed growth of these economies. Already facing a formidable challenge from Japan, the US was not about to allow the emergence of new East Asian competitors following the Japanese model of state-led capitalism.

Penalizing Success: the Case of South Korea

Korea, the most advanced NIC, was the prime target of the US. Thus the US–Korean economic relationship during the last decade serves as a good case study of the difficulties that are placed in the way of a developing country which threatens to breach the barrier between underdevelopment and development, especially when this is done by means that depart from the classic free-market methods enshrined in the ideology of the status quo powers.

The shift in US policy toward its erstwhile ally was inaugurated during Reagan's visit to Korea in 1983. While he used a highly publicized visit to the demilitarized zone (DMZ) to underscore the anti-communist alliance, he also presented the Koreans with tough demands for 'tariff reduction, elimination of quantitative [import] restrictions, liberalization of services, and improved property rights protection.'[5]

Anti-Dumping Measures and VERs

Following the Reagan visit, US pressure on Korea to change its trade, investment, and production practices mounted steadily. An anti-dumping suit filed by the US television industry in 1983 received the backing of the US Commerce Department, which ordered additional duties on Korean television imports. When Korean TV manufacturers tried to minimize the impact of the anti-dumping order by bringing in color picture tubes to be assembled in the US, the Commerce Department, at the behest of the American manufacturers, issued anti-dumping orders on Korean picture-tube imports.[6] This set of rulings, noted one report, 'dealt a heavy blow to Korean television makers.'[7]

The US coupled the strategic use of anti-dumping suits with a tightening of so-called 'voluntary export restraints' (VERs), or self-imposed quotas adopted by exporting countries under threat of retaliation from the importing country (see Appendix 4). Restrictive quotas placed on Korean textile imports under the Multifiber Agreement (MFA) reduced their rate of growth from 43 per cent per year in the 1970s to less than 1 per cent in the early 1980s. VERs imposed on Korean steel limited imports of this commodity to less than 2 per cent of total steel imports.

But anti-dumping suits and VERs could not prevent Korea's trade surplus with the US from reaching US$9.5 billion in 1987. Not surprisingly, in October of that year, senior US Treasury official David Mulford issued what amounted to a declaration of hostilities against Korea and the other NICs: 'Although the NICs may be regarded as tigers because they are strong, ferocious traders, the analogy has a darker side. Tigers live in the jungle, and by the law of the jungle. They are a shrinking population.'[8]

The screws were tightened in 1988, when the US Treasury accused Taiwan and Korea of manipulating their exchange rates to gain 'unfair competitive advantage' in international trade.[9] The Koreans responded to this new pressure by forcing the appreciation of the won relative to the dollar – a move which made Korean imports more expensive and thus less attractive to US consumers. Between 1986 and 1989, in fact, the won appreciated by more than 40 per cent, resulting in great difficulties for Korean exporters. Testifying to the effectiveness of currency warfare, a top Korean textile executive complained: 'We can absorb wage increases but we can't take any more appreciation.'[10]

In 1989 Korea, together with Taiwan, Singapore, and Hong Kong, was knocked off the list of countries eligible for inclusion in the General System of Preferences (GSP), which extends preferential tariff treatment to imports from Third World countries in order to assist their development.

The '301' Offensive

A more important development was the US threat to place Korea on the 'priority watch list' under the much-dreaded 'Super 301 section' of the Omnibus Trade and Competitiveness Act of 1988, which required the US Trade Representative to take retaliatory action against those deemed to be unfair traders. Under Super 301, the US authorities broadly defined trade relations to include Korea's foreign investment regime, which indicated a strategy of using the threat of trade retaliation as a means of changing not just Korea's trading behavior but other economic practices as well. This strategy of pressing on multiple points resulted in the US–Korea Super 301 Agreement of May 1989, under which Korea agreed to liberalize its foreign investment regime by expanding the list of sectors open to investment, simplifying investment approval procedures, and removing performance requirements.[11]

By January 1992, about 98 per cent of industrial areas and 62 per cent of service areas had been opened to foreign equity investments.[12] This and other concessions, however, failed to placate US businesses, which continued to complain about 'restrictions on offshore borrowing and deferred payment for imports; arbitrary and burdensome review procedures; restrictions on land acquisition; government review of joint venture contracts (lack of confidentiality).'[13]

Under another provision of the Omnibus Trade Act, the 'Special 301 Clause,' the US placed Korea on the priority watch list for possible retaliation in May 1989. It was downgraded to the 'watch list' in 1990 and 1991, with a 1992 US Commerce Department investigation reporting that 'General statistics on intellectual property-related arrests, prosecutions, fines, and incarcerations in Korea demonstrate that enforcement efforts continued to improve.'[14] Beyond tighter enforcement, the US government was able to secure for American companies the Koreans' agreement to extend 'retroactive protection that in some cases exceeded the protection afforded to Korean firms.'[15] However, this concession and greater efforts to penalize unauthorized cloners of US computers and other products did not prevent Korea from being upgraded once more to the priority watch list in 1992, after intense lobbying by US-dominated bodies such as the Pharmaceutical Manufacturers' Association and the International Intellectual Property Rights Alliance.

By the early 1990s the US economic offensive had ballooned into an all-encompassing assault that targetted, among other sectors, agriculture, telecommunications, maritime services, financial services, the fishing industry, cosmetics, and government procurement practices. Even health inspection regulations were denounced by the US as imposing 'numerous barriers that prohibit access or inhibit port clearance procedures without a sound scientific basis.'[16]

Cultural Adjustment

When Koreans tried to launch their own modest version of a 'Buy America Campaign' by calling on Koreans to shun overconsumption and practice frugality, the US cried 'Foul!' In one instance, a comic book distributed to Korean children by the Agricultural Cooperatives Federation, which urged them to patronize Korean food products, evoked a raging response, with a member of the US Trade Representative's Office fulminating that 'Everybody who is anybody in the Korean government will hear from us [about the book's] outrageous rhetoric.'[17]

The thrust of US strategy was, in fact, to extend the definition of 'trade barrier' to include a people's propensity to save money and limit consumption. The implications of this move for Korean behavior were summed up in an interesting fashion by one analyst:

> Korean parents today still talk to their children about the *bori gogei* of their early years. *Bori gogei* can be directly translated as 'barley hill.' It represents the difficult period of finding food which occurred in the spring when remaining food from the previous year's autumn harvest usually ran out and was not replenished until the spring barley harvest came in the summer. Consequently, many people used to starve around this time and most Koreans experienced great difficulty in this period of great scarcity.

Today, the problem of absolute poverty, as represented by the *bori gogei* phenomenon has virtually disappeared from the Korean scene and the younger generation only reads or hears about *bori gogei* from books or stories told by their elders. Within the time span of a single generation, Koreans saw their economy move from the status of a developing country to a newly industrializing nation. Now they are about to see their economy attain the status of an industrially advanced country. Koreans' way of thinking, however, could not move as fast as the nation's material advancement. While this may be a blessing, it could become a hindrance when it comes to making the necessary structural adjustments.[18]

Dismantling Agriculture

Although Korea was pressed hard on many fronts, it was in agricultural policy that the US trade assault was most destructive in terms of its impact.

With US agricultural subsidies encouraging massive overproduction by American farmers, renewed pressure on Korea to open up its agricultural market completely developed in the mid-1980s, focused on cigarettes, beef, and rice. This revival of demands to open up agriculture completely came on the heels of two decades of US dumping – through such programs as PL-480 or 'Food for Peace,' a system of subsidized exports tied to development programs – that had contributed in a major way to the erosion of Korea's agricultural base.

Between 1973 and 1983, for instance, grain imports – particularly wheat, corn, and beans – skyrocketed by almost 300 per cent.[19] The lower prices triggered by these imports discouraged domestic production and dropped the self-sufficiency ratio between 1965 and 1983 from 27 per cent to 6 per cent for wheat, from 36 per cent to 2.7 per cent for corn, and from 100 per cent to 25.7 per cent for beans. Indeed, as one analyst claims, 'imports of wheat and cotton from the US have already resulted in the disappearance of Korean farms growing those crops.'[20]

Korea is now the third largest importer of US agricultural products, with imports rising from US$1.8 billion in 1986 to $5 billion by the end of 1991.[21] Indeed, on a per capita basis, Korea now consumes more US farm products than any other foreign nation.[22] Half of Korea's total food imports and 60 per cent of its grain imports come from the United States.[23] When it comes to certain strategic commodities, US trade dominance is even more marked: the United States provides 95–100 per cent of Korea's soybean imports, 74 per cent of its wheat imports, and 70 per cent of its cotton imports.[24]

South Korean demonstrators protesting the visit of President Clinton in Seoul, July, 1993. The farmers are opposed to opening South Korea's rice markets to US imports. (AP/Wide World Photos)

In short, there is very little truth in the image of Korea as a closed agricultural market that is propagated by the US press. In fact, severe competition from imports has contributed to the increasing unattractiveness of farming as an occupation and to the rapid depopulation of the countryside.

Renewed US trade pressure in the mid-1980s threatened to cut off the Korean farmers' last avenues of retreat. This was illustrated forcefully by the opening up of the tobacco market in 1988. Upon reducing trade barriers to US cigarettes, the Korean government encouraged farmers to shift production to other crops, such as red peppers. But an almost 10 per cent increase in fields planted with peppers drastically lowered the market price, resulting in vast unsold stocks and bankruptcy for many farmers.

The mood of desperation that developed was captured by one writer:

As the planting season loomed in the spring of 1989, farmers were confused: 'Hey,' they asked each other, 'what are we going to plant?' We have to plant rice no matter what, but wheat has been a lost cause for some time – imported soybeans have grabbed more than 80 per cent of that market; a few years ago, the garlic market was hot, but seed garlic is in short supply now and western cigarette imports have already forced reductions in tobacco acreage. We just don't have a crop to plant. In the end, the farmers reached the inescapable conclusion that they were caught in a vicious cycle that runs like this: 'First, a crop is opened to imports, which causes a collapse of that crop. That triggers, in turn, mass flight to another crop, which causes over-production, which causes the bottom to drop out of prices. Which causes penniless farmers.'[25]

The US, however, was unrelenting. From tobacco, its attention shifted to beef. Under pressure, the Korean government first allowed the importation of 14,500 tons of beef to meet 10 per cent of domestic demand in 1988, then raised the quota to 50,000 tons in 1989 and 58,000 tons in 1990. These concessions have resulted in imports accounting for 60 per cent of all beef consumed in Korea.[26] Still the US has been far from placated, and recently it has pressed for a fixed increase in beef imports at the rate of 20 per cent of the previous year's imports between 1993 and 1997. And the US Commerce Department has issued what is tantamount to an ultimatum: 'In 1997 Korea should have a tariff-only regime for beef.'[27]

A dislocation greater than that visited on tobacco farmers is likely to ensue with the deprotectionization of beef. Since foreign beef can be sold for as low as a quarter of the domestic price, liberalization is likely to bankrupt a substantial number of the almost 50 per cent of Korean farmers who depend in varying degrees on raising cattle.[28]

Rice is the ultimate prize of the US agricultural lobby. Given its central role in Korean agriculture, however, any significant opening of the rice market will lead to massive dislocation, since foreign rice can be sold at five to seven times less than the price of locally produced rice.[29] As one report notes, 'Once the market is opened,

Korean rice would have no chance of competing.'[30] And that would translate into sure bankruptcy for most of the 7 million farmers – 16 per cent of the workforce – engaged in agriculture, as 92 per cent of them derive more than half of their income from rice production.[31]

Given the contrast between Korean agrarian realities and the US case, where only 1.6 per cent of the workforce is engaged in agriculture, there was a great deal of merit in Korea's National Agricultural Cooperatives Federation's (NACF) plea to President George Bush to accord rice special treatment in US–Korean trade relations, since

> it is a crop of paramount importance to our farmers. Because of our climate, most Korean farmers are engaged in rice cultivation, which takes place on more than 60 per cent of arable land, and provides more than 50 per cent of farm income. Rice is the life blood of Korean farmers. As one of the basic foodstuffs for the Korean people, rice is essential for food security, conservation of the land, and maintenance of rural society.[32]

Free trade, the NACF analysis concludes, 'reflects only the interests of the agricultural exporting countries while neglecting the special conditions in other countries.'[33]

It was, however, unlikely that such pleas would prevent the dismantling of Korean agriculture, for US trade negotiators knew that Korean technocrats had designated agriculture as the sacrificial lamb in a defensive strategy whose overriding goal was to keep the US market open to Korean manufactured exports.

Unilateralism Universalized

The US trade offensive was eminently successful, with South Korea's trade surplus with the United States of US$9.5 billion in 1987, turning into a deficit of $335 million in 1991. Korea was the United States' prime target; indeed, given Korea's lack of retaliatory clout, the US treated it far more harshly than Japan, which had the capacity to hit back effectively. Korea was not the only Asian NIC or 'near-NIC' which became the target of the US trade offensive. As Marcus Noland of the Institute of International Economics points out,

> The current US economic policy toward the Pacific Area developing countries is distinguished by a heavy reliance on bilateral, and public, action to attempt to solve trade disputes. This policy enables the United States to unilaterally set the agenda according to its priorities,

and because of its bilateral orientation, may help the United States extract concessions from its trade partners.[34]

As noted above, Taiwan, Singapore, and Hong Kong lost their GSP status in 1989. The US forced Taiwan to revalue its currency to make its products more expensive to US consumers, subjected a number of its electronics exports to additional duties on anti-dumping grounds, imposed tight limits on its garment and textile exports, and placed it on the Special 301 watch list.

Indonesia was also put on the Special 301 watch list for prohibiting foreign film distributors from directly importing or distributing their films in the country. Meanwhile, Thailand lost up to US$644 billion in GSP benefits following the US Department of Commerce's determination that it 'did not fully provide adequate and effective intellectual property protection.'[35] Indeed, Thailand was designated a 'priority foreign country' under Special 301, meaning it was a step away from US trade retaliation.

Beyond East Asia, Brazil and India received the dubious honor of being two of the three countries – the third was Japan – placed on the first priority watch list for 'Super 301' issued by the United States. Indeed, by the middle of 1990, of the 32 cases of alleged unfair trade initiated by the United States Trade Representative (USTR), over half were directed at Third World countries.[36]

Not even the poorest countries were exempt from punitive action from the United States: Papua New Guinea, a novice at industrialization, was subjected to anti-dumping harassment, while Myanmar (Burma), Fiji, and Bangladesh saw their textile and garment exports to the US subjected to tight MFA restrictions. The implications of these actions were noted by prominent World Bank economist Ann Krueger: 'The recent spectacle of the United States imposing Multifiber Arrangement restrictions on Bangladesh's exports to the United States was grossly inconsistent with the stated American concern for Bangladesh's development.'[37]

Aggressive trade tactics directed at all comers gave the 'free-market' administrations of Ronald Reagan and George Bush the distinction of being the most protectionist since the days of Herbert Hoover. (See Appendix 4 for import restraints imposed by the US from 1980 to 1991.) The Clinton presidency has gladly inherited this legacy; indeed, it shows indications of becoming even more extreme than its Republican predecessors. The Koreans had a taste of protectionism Clinton-style in their first trade talks with the new administration in February 1993, when US trade representative Mickey Kantor demanded that they immediately mount a search-and-destroy operation for some 1.6 million unauthorized copies of video and audio tapes produced before 1987, the year that Korea's new copyright law went into effect.[38]

Actions like this led UNCTAD to brand US trade strategy as 'unilateralism' and 'forced negotiation.' If institutionalized, the agency warned, US unilateralism

> would have very adverse consequences for developing countries, which do not have sufficient leverage to dissuade a powerful trading partner from such practices. Moreover, the rule of law in international trade would be unavoidably weakened, and the results that may emerge from the Uruguay Round would be inevitably compromised.[39]

GATT as a Weapon

In the eyes of many developing countries, however, the present Uruguay Round of GATT (General Agreement on Tariffs and Trade) does not hold out the promise of being an improvement over US unilateralism. For the Round seeks to bring new areas of the international economy apart from commodity trade into a regulatory framework that favors the United States and other Northern countries and may have crippling effects on the efforts of the South to develop. These areas are Trade-Related Intellectual Property Rights (TRIPs), Trade-Related Investment Measures (TRIMs), and Services.

TRIPS ...

In the negotiations on TRIPs, the United States and other Northern countries have aggressively sought to restrict the diffusion of technological advances to the Third World by strengthening the international regime governing patents, trademarks, and royalties favoring Northern multinational corporations. The North also seeks to extend patenting to living matter developed by biotechnology. This is a matter of no small concern to the South, for while developments in biotechnology are greatly dependent on the freely available genetic resources of the Third World, the patented products developed from these resources are likely to be sold to Southern farmers at high prices by Northern corporate patent-holders.

The draft agreement on TRIPs, according to an analysis carried out for UNCTAD, shows that '[m]ost of the major areas of tension between developed and Third World countries have been clearly resolved ... on the side of the former.'

Thus, patentability was forcefully extended to food, micro-organisms, pharmaceuticals, chemicals, and the processes to produce them. Only diagnostic, therapeutic and surgical methods for treatment of humans and animals, animals (except micro-organisms) and biological (except microbiological) processes to produce plants and animals were excluded from forceful patentability; it was established, on the other hand, that plant varieties could be protected by either patents or an effective *sui generis* system.[40]

Moreover, a generalized minimum patent protection of 20 years was granted, which included controversial privileges contested by Third World countries, such as a multinational firm's exclusive right to import its biotechnological products into a country. Protection for layout-designs of semiconductors was increased from eight to ten years. Punitive border regulations against products judged to be violating international property rights were adopted. Finally, the burden of proof was placed on the presumed violator in cases involving process patents.[41]

In short, the TRIPs regime represents what UNCTAD describes as a 'premature strengthening of the international intellectual property system ... that favors monopolistically controlled innovation over broad-based diffusion.'[42] And its likely consequence would be to limit the possibility of an 'imitative path of technological development' based on methods such as reverse engineering, the adaptation of foreign technology to local conditions, and the improvement of existing innovations.[43] It was precisely the creative employment of these methods that produced a Japan, a South Korea, and a Taiwan.

... and TRIMs

In the area of TRIMs, the US sought to do away with mechanisms used by Third World countries to ensure that foreign investment contributes to national development. These included investment requirements that specified a maximum percentage of foreign equity ownership, local content regulations that mandated minimum levels of local material to be used in a product, and investment rules requiring foreign investors to export part or all of their production.

While no consensus on TRIMs emerged, the proposal of GATT's director-general, Arthur Dunkel, sought the dismantling by developing countries, within five to seven years, of local-content specifications, export requirements, and other development-oriented investment mechanisms.[44] On the other hand, the proposal makes no mention of measures to curb the trade-distorting activities of multinational investors, such as transfer pricing, or artificially depressing export prices to subsidiaries, and tying purchases to selected external suppliers. The distorting effects on trade of these multinational mechanisms are great, since over half of international trade is transnational and probably two-thirds of that is from one subsidiary or branch of a corporation to another.[45] The implications of this reality for the theory and practice of free trade are drawn out by economist Bill Rosenberg:

> [W]hen people talk about international 'free trade,' meaning trade at a price set on an open market, at least a third of world trade is immune from that because its price is simply an arbitrary value in the books of some transnational. Transnationals want 'free trade' simply because it frees them from government intervention – they don't want free trade in the conventional sense.[46]

Opening up the Service Sector

In the critical area of services, the draft agreement established the principle of 'national treatment,' or giving foreign investors the same treatment accorded to domestic providers of services.[47] Securing this principle has been of critical interest to multinational corporations, because in recent years between half and two-thirds of the growth in foreign investment has been in services, including transport, construction, telecommunications, financial services, and legal services.[48] Moreover, its adoption is likely to weaken the negotiating leverage of Southern governments which wish to preserve the time-honored principle of preferential treatment of citizens engaged in the provision of services. Given the tremendous resources of multinationals, the principle of national treatment, according to Martin Khor of the Third World Network, is likely to 'dislocate the smaller local enterpreneurs and professionals and curb the development of a domestic service sector.'[49]

Double Standards

While the areas of great interest to Northern transnationals have been largely resolved in their favor in the GATT, there has been little movement in textiles, where change toward freer markets would benefit the South. While a consensus on dismantling the Multifiber Agreement has been reached, the draft text proposes a very gradual phaseout process which allows for 49 per cent of textile imports in 1990 to remain outside GATT discipline by the year 2000.[50] Effectively, what this means, according to UNCTAD, is that the agreement will not affect major restrictions until the beginning of the next century. Moreover, 'there will be very generous transitional safeguards, including country-selective quotas ... [which contradict] two basic principles of GATT: the most-favored nation clause and the use of quotas only as emergency balance-of-payments devices.'[51]

Riddled throughout with double standards, the GATT draft agreement stands out as a testament both to the resurgence of the economic power of the North and the increasing helplessness of the South. Rather than lead to a future where free trade results in global prosperity, as its advocates promise, the GATT is much more likely to result in what Chakravarthi Raghavan described as 'recolonialization' of the Third World.[52]

'The One and Only Path'

Unilateralism and the GATT, in short, are two faces of the same process of resubordination directed at those countries which threaten to make the breakthrough to developed status. In much the same way that structural adjustment programs seek to contain the poorer countries of the South, the GATT and aggressive unilateral trade policy aim to roll back the NICs and aspiring NICs. Understandably, 'structural adjustment' is a term that South Koreans increasingly use to describe what the United States wants to do with their economy.

For the United States wishes to accomplish more than the rectification of trade imbalances. It seeks to reinforce a set of global economic practices whose observance would favor the continued dominance of the status quo powers, in particular the United States. The drive to institutionalize these practices, which come under the rubric of 'free markets' and 'free trade,' is designed to make other models of capitalist development illegitimate. It is directed, in particular, at those development strategies in which the state – through planning, industrial targetting, protecting markets, favoring local investors, or engaging in production itself – spearheads the process of development and makes 'catching up with the North' a real possibility. It aims, in fact, to make it very difficult for new Japans, new South Koreas, and new Taiwans to emerge from the South.

Adjusting America

The tales [Ronald Reagan] loved most as a boy and man were stories of individualist heroes. [H]e never noticed that it was the government that had protected these frontier heroes, set aside land for homes and schools, built telegraph lines and underwritten construction of an inter-continental railway system.

—Lou Cannon, *Washington Post* White House correspondent, *President Reagan: the Role of a Lifetime* (New York: Simon and Schuster, 1991)

What in the Bible says we should have a better living standard than others? We have to give a bit of it back.

—Walter Joelson, chief economist of General Electric, quoted in Kevin Phillips, *Boiling Point: Democrats, Republicans, and the Decline of Middle-Class Prosperity* (New York: Random House, 1993)

To the free-market ideologues who came to power with the Reagan administration in 1981, the rollback of the South was part of a broader strategy that involved the defeat of communism globally and the dismantling of the New Deal compromise in the United States. Domestic rollback was just as central to Reaganism's agenda as the global reassertion of US hegemony, and its main thrust was to end the fragile social contract between big capital and big labor that had emerged out of the Great Depression, in the belief that this would release the entrepreneurial energy which would reinvigorate American capitalism.

Political Economy of the New Deal State

The basis for the New Deal or neo-New Deal 'social contract,' which reigned roughly from the late 1930s to the late 1970s, was the mutual benefit derived by big labor and big capital from Keynesian policies imposed by big government. These policies, which consisted principally of the manipulation of fiscal and monetary mechanisms to assure stable economic growth, were followed not only by Democrats dependent on the labor union vote but even by socially conservative Republicans like Richard Nixon, one of whose best-known declarations during his presidency was 'We are all Keynesians now.' Keynesianism in practice had liberal and conservative variants, with the former stressing growth and the latter the containment of inflation. The two variants, however, shared the same assumption that both the economic health of American capitalism and the social well-being of the country rested on the maintenance of mass purchasing power at a high level.

Why did corporate capital accommodate itself to state-managed Keynesian capitalism? Because this framework promised stable growth and rising profitability, says Ray Marshall, secretary of labor during the Carter administration:

> A serious problem for mass-production companies was to control markets and prices in order to justify the large investments required for these systems. These firms therefore worked out oligopolistic arrangements to avoid price competition and adjusted to change mainly by varying output and employment while holding prices relatively constant.
>
> There was, however, another problem. Once they stabilized the prices of their products, the mass-production companies experienced cyclical instability because production tended to outrun consumption at administered prices. The industrialized market economy countries fixed this problem through so-called 'Keynesian' monetary-fiscal policies which manipulated government spending and interest rates to generate enough total demand to keep the system operating at relatively low levels of unemployment.[1]

Labor unions, collective bargaining, unemployment compensation, and social security were justified as institutions necessary to sustain purchasing power. And though they were initially brought into this system with great reluctance on their part,

> oligopolistic companies could see the wisdom of providing purchasing power, especially when it became clear that unions and collective bargaining were not really going to challenge their control of the system – they were merely going to codify work force practices and protect workers from some of the most arbitrary company practices. The unemployment compensation system

also helped companies maintain their work force by, in effect, supplementing wages during layoffs.[2]

Completing the political economy of the New Deal or neo-New Deal state was a regime of moderately high taxes, which was channelled both to massive defense spending in order to contain global communism and to social expenditures such as social security and welfare in order to buy social peace domestically. Cementing this structure was the ideology of containment liberalism that, as noted earlier, combined anti-communism in foreign policy with liberal domestic social and economic strategies.

Collapse of the Social Contract

By the early 1970s, however, the social contract that underpinned this system was fraying. Corporations complained about high tax rates imposed by the state, which they claimed diverted resources from reinvestment and from research and development (R&D). But even more central to US corporate capital's disaffection was what it claimed to be an increasing competitive disadvantage faced by US-based production in an era marked by the rapid globalization of markets and production.

Under conditions of global production and globalized markets, the relatively high wages of US workers had become a stumbling block to competitiveness, asserted the corporations, and they pointed to an international situation of widely disparate wage rates in which the average monthly income of a US worker was US$1220 in 1972, while Taiwanese workers made an average of only $45, South Korean workers $68, Singaporean workers $60, and workers in Hong Kong $82.

If expensive US labor was the problem, then cheap foreign labor was the solution, and US capital voted with its feet in a dramatic fashion. From 1965 to 1980 private US investment abroad rose fourfold, from US$50 billion to $214 billion.[3] While much of this investment was directed at penetrating local markets, a growing part of it was devoted to producing commodities for the US market. For instance, the portion of sales of US multinational affiliates in the Asia-Pacific region which was exported to the US market rose from 10 per cent in 1966 to more than 25 per cent by 1977.[4] As Joseph Grunwald and Kenneth Flamm point out, this movement of capital in search of cheap labor marked a new stage in the evolution of the world capitalist system [in which] the operations of US multinational firms seem to have switched, on a fairly large scale for the first time, to overseas production of manufactured exports for the home market.[5]

The switch to overseas production was especially marked in highly competitive, highly profitable industries such as consumer electronics, where it resulted in the 'hollowing out' of the US-based industry. In the case of the television industry, the effort to compete with high-quality Japanese TV sets flooding the US market led American firms to relocate most of their operations to Third World sites such as Mexico, Taiwan, and Singapore in the 1960s. By the mid-1970s, although some 20 per cent of the black-and-white TV receivers sold in the US were still nominally produced there, 'substantial imports of subassemblies and parts from locations in Taiwan and Mexico were incorporated into these sets.'[6] This trend was repeated in the color television industry: the emigration to Mexico and East Asia of key manufacturing operations resulted in the value of overseas-produced subassemblies and parts rising from 23 per cent to more than 90 per cent of total components used by US firms.[7] Not surprisingly, jobs in the US television manufacturing industry fell by 50 per cent between 1966 and 1970, and by another 30 per cent between 1971 and 1975.[8]

This corporate discontent with one of the pillars of the New Deal state – a high-wage labor force – had momentous consequences. Ever since the 1930s, there had been vociferous demands by free-market ideologues, including University of Chicago economists Friedrich Van Hayek and Milton Friedman, to dismantle the New Deal state and dump its Keynesian ideology. These ideas, however, could only make headway in the late 1970s and 1980s because corporate capital had detached itself from the New Deal modus vivendi. Corporate capital hitched itself to the rising star of free-market economics, and it did so with the knowledge that while the Reaganite ideologues spoke trenchantly of 'letting the free market work its magic,' few of them saw corporate monopolies as the villain. Rather, big capital was, for the most part, regarded by the rising Republican right as a force that had to be liberated from a misguided alliance with big labor and big government. Indeed, far from deriding the corporate monopolies, the Reaganites saw the concentration of wealth as a positive thing, for only with the incentive of being able to accumulate and enjoy more wealth would individuals be made to invest more in productive activity, thus keeping the engine of economic growth chugging along.

The political and economic elites of the United States were not alone in abandoning Keynesianism. Indeed, Margaret Thatcher and British capital provided a role model for the Reaganites, with their 'monetarist' assault on the welfare state. And throughout the 1980s and early 1990s, the 'conservative revolution' spread throughout Europe, leading to the ousting of social democrats from power in Sweden and, in the case of the socialists in France, their defensive adoption of liberal market policies.

Reaganism: from Ideology to Policy

The first years of triumphant Reaganism were marked by a glorification of capitalist enterprise unparalleled since the 1920s. This belief in the capitalist as the heroic saver and investor – which was the cornerstone of 'supply-side economics' – was translated into policy during Reagan's first term, taking the form of deep cuts in federal taxes on individual incomes, businesses, gifts, and estates. The Economic Recovery Tax Act of 1981, the Tax Equity and Fiscal Responsibility Act of 1982, and the Social Security Amendments of 1983 reduced personal taxes by US$117 billion but led to an increase of $11 billion in social security taxes.[9] The result was a windfall for the rich: the tax share of the top 1 per cent of the population fell by 14 per cent, while that of the bottom 10 per cent rose by 28 per cent.[10]

This upward redistribution of income through tax reform was accompanied by an assault on the interventionist powers of government at both the federal and state levels, under the slogan of 'balancing the budget.' This was, however, a very selective attack, for it targeted those agencies and programs that managed the 'social safety net' created by the New Deal state but strengthened the military–industrial complex designed to roll back global communism. By 1985, non-defense procurement was down US$16 billion from 1981 levels, funds for entitlement programs (such as food stamps, employment and training programs, Aid to Families with Dependent Children [AFDC], and social security benefits) were cut by close to $30 billion, but defense spending was $35 billion greater.[11]

With resources from the federal government drying up, state governments followed Washington's lead during the later Reagan years and throughout the Bush era. In 1991 and 1992 alone, a phenomenal 40 states drastically dismantled social safety nets via 'welfare reform' and similar draconian measures.[12] By the end of the Republican period, the combination of federal and state cuts had resulted in a real cut in welfare benefits (AFDC and food stamps) of about 40 per cent from their levels in the early 1970s.[13]

Perhaps even most drastically affected by the fiscal cutoff were the cities, which were already suffering from an erosion of their tax base owing to white middle-class flight to the suburbs during the 1960s and 1970s. By the end of the Reagan–Bush era, federal aid to the cities had plummeted by 60 per cent from its level in 1981.[14] The upsurge of crime, spread of drugs, and consolidation of inner-city poverty were among the predictable results.

The third major policy thrust was deregulation. Many populists drawn to Reagan expected that this would mean the breaking up of monopolies. In practice, however, in services like banking, law, medicine, and cable television, deregulation led not to lower prices through greater competition but to skyrocketing charges, owing to professional solidarity or collusion. And in airlines, trucking, and railroads, deregulation became a means not of breaking up monopolies but of doing away with obstacles to corporate mergers and acquisitions.[15]

The fourth key prong of Reaganomics was aimed at breaking the resistance of labor to corporate capital's drive for greater freedom to reduce costs and increase profitability. In close cooperation with the administration, the Federal Reserve Board headed by Paul Volcker adopted a tight monetary policy in 1981. The ostensible objective was to whip inflation, but the strategic objective was to break labor by triggering a deep recession. Just as in the Third World, anti-inflationary rhetoric became the spearhead of structural adjustment in the United States. And, as in the Third World, adjustment savaged the working class. According to economists Bennett Harrison and Barry Bluestone:

> [For] business, the deep recession did precisely what it was designed to do. With more than ten million people unemployed in 1982, it was impossible for organized labor to maintain wage standards, let alone raise them. Reductions in wages rippled from one industry to the next and from the center of the country outward. The real average weekly wage fell by more than 8 per cent between 1979 and 1982, and failed to recover at all in the next five years. Essentially, with wage growth arrested by unemployment, what growth occurred during the Reagan period redounded mostly to the profits side of the capital–labor ledger.[16]

More forcefully, Reagan sought confrontation with organized labor. This opportunity was provided by the Professional Air Controllers' Union (PATCO) strike in 1981, which ended with the wholesale dismissal of all the strikers and the dissolution of their union.

The PATCO solution sent a message to both the private and public sectors that it was open season on labor. Labor-management relations in the next few years were marked by a management offensive consisting of aggressive union-busting, prevention of unionization through right-to-work laws, replacement of full-time with part-time workers, wage and benefit 'give-backs' under threat of plant closure, and increased subcontracting of work. As University of California labor expert Harley Shaiken noted:

> We've always seen aggressive management in many industries. What's different now is that a number of companies who for most of the last 40 years operated on the basis of a certain social contract are redefining the terms of that contract. It isn't just a back-alley machine shop with 200 workers going after its union. It's AT&T violating seniority rules. It's Caterpillar threatening to replace its work force ... Public companies that would have shunned these tactics a decade ago are now using them.[17]

The successful assault on organized labor was apparent in wage trends: between 1979 and 1989 the hourly wages of 80 per cent of the workforce declined, with the wage of the typical (or median) worker falling by nearly 5 per cent in real terms.[18] Male workers with 12 or fewer years of schooling lost the most ground, with their hourly wages falling by 20 per cent.[19]

Wage inequality between highly skilled and less skilled workers also increased, and about a fifth of the total rise in wage inequality probably stemmed from the decline in union membership as a result of what one observer called the 'Darwinian labor markets of the 1980s.'[20]

The Coming of the 'Service Economy'

Even as the corporations sought to lower US wage costs by breaking organized labor, they consolidated the trend of shifting significant sections of their manufacturing operations to Third World countries whose protection of labor was weak, encouraged by Republican rhetoric that glorified the pursuit of profits and downgraded corporate responsibility to the community. This translated into the continuing loss of millions of actual and potential manufacturing jobs that had served as the 'tickets to middle-class status for two generations of postwar blue-collar workers, a process that limited socioeconomic disparity.'[21]

By the early 1990s, the hollowing out of manufacturing began to impact on the white-collar work force. With smaller blue-collar contingents to manage, and quality managers, engineers, and designers available at much lower cost in Third World countries, US corporations, from IBM to GM, 'downsized' not just white-collar ranks but middle and upper-middle management too, leading to the 1991–3 recession's trademark of managers and highly skilled professionals joining semi-skilled and unskilled workers on the unemployment lines. Recession and job migration drove down white-collar wages and benefits by over 2 per cent between 1987 and 1988, while the hourly wage of college-educated members of the workforce fell by over 3 per cent between 1987 and 1991.[22]

Even when advances in flexible automation began to make production in the United States cost-competitive with labor-intensive production in the Third World, corporations used the new techniques not to upgrade the role of American workers in the production process, but to displace them further. Throughout the 1980s, corporations broke down the power of labor by substituting high-tech machines for well-paid skilled workers. The sophisticated knowledge that controlled the machines was concentrated in a highly educated professional elite, while the rest of the workforce was reduced to a deskilled mass of 'keypunchers.' As Lenny Siegel, an authority on high-tech industries, describes it:

> The downgrading of work is no accident. Nor is it the necessary result of the new technologies. Rather, employers have chosen to use the new computer technology to de-skill their work force. The knowledge and experience that it formerly took to run machine tools in auto plants and cash registers at fast-food restaurants have been programmed into the equipment.
>
> The clerk who greets one at a MacDonald's no longer needs to know how to figure change, memorize prices, or even write orders. The computerized cash register does it all. Some even substitute symbols – such as a drawing of hamburger – for words. Such employers can hire unskilled, non-English-speaking workers, and they can save money by paying extremely low wages.[23]

Unwilling to stem the export or shrinkage of manufacturing jobs, free-market ideologues made a virtue out of necessity by proclaiming that the US was entering a higher state of capitalist development: the 'service economy.' But the truth was that most services were low-value-added activities, thus contributing significantly less than manufacturing to economic dynamism. Except for a few job categories, such as that of advanced programmer, university professor, or bank executive, service sector jobs were poorly paid. The 'sad truth,' noted

Senator Lawton Chiles of Florida, was that 'jobs paying below the poverty level are growing faster than any other kind.'[24] At the last count, 58 per cent of the 8 million new jobs created during the 1980s paid less than US$11,611 for a family of four.[25] Moreover, as Republican analyst Kevin Phillips noted, the wage-and-salary differentials in the services were shockingly wide:

> As service industries took over, with education and talent counting for less, much wider cleavage would be the rule – a bottom stratum of low paid $4.50 and $6.50-an-hour employees supporting an upper echelon of senior executives making forty, fifty, or sixty times as much.[26]

NAFTA: Securing a Cheap Labor Preserve

The replacement of manufacturing and high-skilled jobs by low-paid service jobs is likely to accelerate if the US Congress approves the North American Free Trade Agreement, which would eliminate tariff barriers to the flow of goods in Mexico, Canada, and the United States. Already, some 600,000 jobs that would otherwise have been located in the US have been created by affiliates of US corporations operating in northern Mexico, attracted by wages that are between one-tenth and one-fourteenth as high as US wages and a customs regime that places a tariff only on the value added by the assembly by Mexican labor of manufactures made up of US-sourced components.[27]

By knocking down remaining tariff restrictions and guaranteeing the 'rights of foreign investors into an international agreement that future Mexican governments would find difficult or impossible to change,'[28] NAFTA is corporate America's effort to guarantee the existence for an indefinite period of a cheap-labor preserve. For as John Pearlman, chairman of the Zenith Electronic Corporation, predicts, 'it could be years before the gap with American wages narrows significantly.'[29]

If concluded, a NAFTA agreement, according to one study, is likely to promote the migration of 290,000 to 490,000 more US jobs over the next 10 years.[30] A significant number of these jobs will not be low-skilled assembly jobs but skilled positions with salaries at a fraction of US rates. As one report on the Ford engine plant in Chihuahua, Mexico, asserted,

> in the 1980s, corporate America realized that low wages could attract not only unskilled people, but also educated applicants in cities like Chihuahua that boasts many graduates from public universities and technical schools. The Ford pay, slightly above the norm

in Mexico, is deeply below American levels, where a manufacturing worker's average wage is $11 an hour and an engineer newly out of school commands $25,000 to $30,000 a year as a starting salary. By comparison, Esquiel De Luna, a 20-year-old sophomore in electronic engineering at the Institute of Technology here, expects to earn $400 a month – $4,800 a year – at one of the factories after graduation, and work up to $12,000 annually in three or four years. 'I would not take a first job as an engineer for less than $400,' he said.[31]

Justifying the corporate strategy of regaining competitiveness by exploiting such wage differentials, Walter Joelson, chief economist at General Electric, said: 'Let's talk about the differences in living standards rather than wages. What in the Bible says we should have a better living standard than others? We have to give a bit of it back.'[32]

The 'Third Worldization' of America

The double squeeze by corporate America and Republican Washington, in fact, forced Americans to give back quite a bit. The 1980s ended with the top 20 per cent of the population having the largest share of total income, while the bottom 60 per cent had the lowest share of total income ever recorded.[33] Indeed, within the top 20 per cent, the gains of the Reagan–Bush period were concentrated in the top 1 per cent, whose income grew by 63 per cent between 1980 and 1989, capturing over 53 per cent of the total income growth among all families. Meanwhile, the bottom 60 per cent of families actually experienced a decline in income.[34] (See Appendices 5 and 6 for changes in distribution of US income and wealth.)

The same radically regressive trends were evident in wealth holdings, which were even more concentrated than income:

[I]n 1989, the top 1 per cent of families earned 14.1% total income, yet owned 38.3% of total net worth and 50.3% of net financial assets. The wealth distribution has also become more unequal over time. The wealth holdings of the richest 0.5% of families grew by one percentage point over the entire 21-year period, 1962–83, but grew by four times as much in just six years between 1983 and 1989. Meanwhile, the bottom 60% of families had lower wealth holdings in 1989 than 1983.[35]

The trends revealed a middle class that was losing ground. Median family incomes for 1990 and 1991 dropped to their levels of the late 1970s when adjusted for taxes and inflation.[36] But even more alarming

was the fact that these trends translated into greater poverty and hunger among the more vulnerable sectors of the population.

The percentage of whites living in poverty rose from 9 per cent in 1979 to 10 per cent in 1989. In the case of Hispanics, the increase was from 22 to 26 per cent, while black poverty remained steady at 31 per cent.[37] While the ratio of black to white incomes did not change much, with black median income remaining at 60 per cent that of whites, the ratio of Hispanic to white median income fell from 69 per cent in 1979 to 65 per cent in 1989.[38] Despite the differences in racial impact, it is clear that the most prominent feature in the Reagan rollback was its class character.

That their circumstances had not declined further with respect to whites according to some social indicators was, of course, cold comfort for blacks, for the inequalities that remained the same or became only slightly more pronounced are nevertheless stark: average black per capita income is now less than 60 per cent that of whites; 13 per cent of blacks are jobless compared with 6 per cent for whites; and the life expectancy of black males is seven years less than that of white males.[39]

By the end of the Republican era, the United States, a congressional study asserted, had become 'the most unequal of modern nations.'[40] Some 20 million Americans were said to be experiencing hunger; 25 million of them – some one in every 10 – were receiving federal food stamps.[41] The child poverty rate, which had risen from 18 per cent in 1980 to 22 per cent in 1991, was the highest among the industrialized countries.[42] Among children in minority groups, the poverty rate was even higher, at almost 50 per cent.[43]

Indeed, structural adjustment Republican-style was beginning to give the US a Third World appearance: rising poverty, widespread homelessness, greater inequality, social polarization. But perhaps it was the condition of infants that most starkly captured the 'Third Worldization' of America. The infant mortality rate for African-Americans now stands at 17.7 infant deaths per 1,000 live births. This figure compares unfavorably not only to those for most other industrial countries but even to figures for some of the developing countries of the Caribbean, such as Jamaica (17.2 per 1,000), Trinidad (16.3), and Cuba (16).[44]

Homeless family in Mendocino County, California, 1989. The 'Reagan Revolution' created pockets of enormous wealth while it marginalized the vast majority, driving the living standards of many Americans to Third World levels. (Evan Johnson, Impact Visuals)

A nine-year-old works in a Brooklyn, New York, garment factory. It is not just the Third World that suffers from child-labor exploitation. (Lina Pallotta, Impact Visuals)

Accelerating Decline

Ironically, an administration pledged to restoring US strength accelerated the decline of US economic power at a time of tougher global competition. This paradox stems from the fact that while they reinforced the global military power of the US and promoted short-term economic growth, administration and corporate policies had disastrous consequences from the perspective of the long-term health of the US economy.

First of all, in order to pursue the Cold War, the Reagan–Bush administrations resorted to massive deficit spending that was largely financed by borrowings from Japan, which had emerged as the United States' prime competitor. By 1992 the deficit came to a record US$400 billion, or 6.8 per cent of GNP. The national debt stood at US$3.5 trillion and was growing by $1 billion daily.

Second, with their worship of the invisible hand of the market as the best shaper of America's economic future and their view of activist government as 'socialist,' the Reagan and Bush administrations eschewed strategic planning and the formulation of an industrial policy. But leaving the corporations to take care of America's industrial future was perhaps the worst way to assure the United States' techno-manufacturing competitiveness. For the greater income that accrued to the corporations from the tax cuts and labor's waning power went not to enhancing America's productive capacity, but mainly to financing corporate takeovers, hothouse speculative activities, junk-bond operations on Wall Street, investment in low-wage sites in Asia and Latin America, and soaring executive pay.

Comparisons with the United States' main competitors underline this. In 1989 Japan invested 23.2 per cent of its GNP in plant and capital equipment and R&D, while the US invested 11.7 per cent.[45] In non-defense R&D spending, US expenditures as a percentage of GNP in the 1980s came to 1.8 per cent, while the figures for West Germany and Japan were 2.6 per cent and 2.8 per cent respectively.[46] It is hardly cause for surprise then that the US, which pioneered the development of most high technologies, has lost the lead to Japan in memory chips, semiconductor manufacturing equipment, robotics, numerically controlled machine tools, optoelectronics, and other strategic areas. Such creative R&D that did exist was confined to the military–industrial establishment, in the fabrication of more sophis-ticated weapons of mass destruction.

Indeed, the knives of the anti-state ideologues cut even the infra-structure outlays so necessary to increasing the productivity of the American economy. By 1990 the non-military portion of the federal budget that was spent on infrastructure was down to 1 per cent, having fallen from almost 7 per cent in the early 1950s.[47] Not surprisingly, one recent congressional report discovered that 35 per cent of the United States' interstate roads will have outlived their useful life in two years' time.[48] '[B]ridges and roads are crumbling,' noted the *New York Times*, 'partly because the nation spends a far smaller fraction of gross domestic product on infrastructure than do Japan and Germany.'[49] This observation can be borne out by New Yorkers who have driven on a German *autobahn* or ridden Japan's incom-parable inter-city rail system.

The 'Human Capital' Question

While the deficit, corporate irresponsibility, and a vacuum in industrial policy have certainly been important factors accounting for the loss of US techno-manufacturing supremacy, probably the most critical has been the failure of the US to develop its human capital – to use a fashionable term for its callous and extremely short-sighted treatment of labor.

In the book *Voltaire's Bastards,* John Ralston Saul advances the thesis that the US corporations' decision to manufacture abroad to take advantage of low wages will ultimately have the same historic significance as ancient Rome's decision to import rather than grow wheat, and Britain's repeal of the Corn Laws and decision to import cheap Indian cotton.[50] The common feature of these decisions was the sacrifice of the welfare of the domestic workforce in the interests of short-term profitability.

Saul's insight gains force if one compares the US solution to the problem of regaining competitiveness to that of Japan and Germany, which are America's prime competitors. Several studies on competitiveness, including the landmark *Machine that Changed the World,* an investigation of the international automobile industry, have made the point that it is not high-tech methods but innovations in the social organization of production that account for the ability of Japan to turn out the nearly 'zero-defect' output which has made it the prime power in the automobile industry.[51] The much-vaunted Japanese teamwork, the initiative of workers in the production process, the constant efforts collectively to upgrade and diversify the work team's skills – all this stems from a system of production where much of the conflict between labor and management has been reduced or softened.

In return for job security, bonuses, and a variety of material and psychic benefits, 'core workers' in the Japanese firm share entrepreneurial risk with management. Since their material benefits are tied to the competitiveness and the status of the corporation, workers have become active participants in promoting innovation that raises productivity. Moreover, hierarchy and authority are blurred within the Japanese firm, with responsibility the more dominant structuring principle. As Koji Matsumoto, a former member of the vaunted Ministry for Trade and Industry (MITI), describes it:

> [T]he Japanese corporate system is structured so that it allows for the coexistence of organizational efficiency and the freedom of those working within it to a far greater degree than the Western system. Alternatively, it has the flexibility to ensure that the efforts made toward achieving this actually bear fruit. Of course, just as there can never be an organization which is wholly dependent on authority, neither can there be an organization which is wholly dependent on initiative. Japanese companies, however, by creating a consensus of interests between the company and the individual,

have been able to achieve true worker participation, something which has been totally unattainable with Western methods.[52]

Commentators like Matsumoto appear to overstate the case, neglecting to mention, for instance, that there is a great difference in the way that the Japanese firm treats its contract workers, as opposed to its 'core workers.' Also, they often fail to appreciate how 'group pressure' can, at times, be as negative in terms of its psychological and physical impact as hierarchical pressure: deaths from overwork are on the increase in Japan. Nevertheless, it is true that most Japanese 'core workers' – the dynamo of the firm – are far less alienated from management than American workers are. Moreover, management knows that non-alienated workers are the key to competitiveness. Strong confirmation of this relationship is provided by one report on the behavior of Japanese automobile companies during the 1993 recession in Japan:

> Avoiding a layoff is part of the Japanese production theology. But it has a point, too. Keeping workers occupied is particularly important for the Toyota system, which in both Japan and the United States emphasizes worker efficiency and multiple skills.
>
> As car sales have waned in Japan's recession, the number of hours Japanese auto workers spend on the job has been cut from an average of 2,300 a year to 1,800, or more than 20 per cent ... Because the Japanese car companies demand a high level of worker participation to maintain high-quality manufacturing, they choose to slow the work rather than to lay off and rehire workers.[53]

According to Daniel Jones, co-author of *The Machine that Changed the World*, 'The Japanese think of workers more as a long-term resource ... [T]he last thing they want to do is hire and fire workers.'[54]

Germany, with its 'social market' economy, has also been careful to cultivate its human resources. The Germans, says Jeffrey Garten, are obsessed with training and retraining workers in order to maintain competitiveness.[55] In contrast to the US, which has almost no vocational training and where upgrading of workers' skills is the responsibility of the individual worker, Germany has an 'unmatched ability to produce skilled workers' via a national apprenticeship system that encompasses most 16 year-olds after their formal schooling. The curriculum and costs of this system are determined and shared by government, firms, and labor unions.[56] While manpower policies in Germany and Japan are by no means identical, Garten contends that their common feature is that workers participate in company decisions. They have a good sense *of their employers' mission and purpose, and their involvement enhances motivation.* Whereas American workers derive their prestige from their salaries, wages, and benefits, in Japan and Germany, status is heavily dependent on the reputation and performance of the companies of which they are a part. Workers identify with their companies and assume they will spend their productive life with them, which the companies also assume. As a result, employers are willing to make investments in their work force to upgrade skills, and workers are motivated to expend the effort to acquire such skills.[57]

In contrast to Japan and Germany, workers in the United States resist suggesting ways to increase productivity since that would be equivalent to 'tying a noose around their own necks.'[58] Indeed, studies of automation have shown that increases in productivity in the US have been accompanied by a reduction in wages, while in Japan they have gone hand-in-hand with a rise in wages.[59] Whereas automation has been used to enhance worker skills in Japan, it has been utilized by American managers to deskill and reduce their workforces.

The contradiction between the enhancement of human capital and the traditional route of greater profitability is but one aspect of the deeper contradiction in labor–management relations in the United States and some other Western countries. This contradiction is perhaps best expressed by the following account:

> Much of the industrial stagnation, weakened competitiveness and declining vitality experienced by these companies stems from their use and control of humans as they would machines, and the blame should rest with the system which has oppressed the freedom of those who work within it. This problem has occurred because, under this system, production efficiency and human freedom are linked antinomically, and the more entrenched the mechanical control of human beings becomes, i.e., the greater the degree of human oppression, the more efficient the production process.[60]

This observation comes not from a Marxist but from an observant ex-MITI official, who comes to the following conclusion: 'Under the economic system that exists in the West ... economic development is accompanied by the devastation of labor and the destruction of a healthy social psyche. This system must therefore be regarded as normal.'[61]

To survive the Japanese challenge, many US firms scrambled in the 1980s to adopt Japanese management techniques, such as 'quality circles' and work teams. Except with Japanese subsidiaries and a few US ventures like Motorola and Xerox, however, these methods have had very limited success in the US. The reason why is evident when one looks at IBM: this corporation is one of the leading advocates of 'total quality management' (TQM),[62] which relies on worker participation, at the same time that it is radically reducing its workforce. The social context of production is the essential stumbling block for most US firms: unless there are indications that management is revising its fundamental relationship with labor – unless, that is, as in Japan, management is seriously bringing in labor as a partner in production – most workers will see the new techniques simply as more sophisticated efforts by corporate capital to raise productivity at their expense.

For the most part, US corporations are meeting the competitive challenge of the 1990s by continuing the strategy of the 1980s: throwing off workers at home and hiring cheap labor abroad. While Japanese firms 'clung with such tenacity to their system of "life-time" employment despite intense pressure to abandon it',[63] even US companies that were experiencing good times, such as Walmart and Procter and Gamble, were embracing downsizing as a basic strategy to maintain profit margins. For instance, Procter and Gamble decided to cut 13,000 jobs in 1993, a year of record earnings.[64] Downsizing resulted in some 2 million layoffs in 1991–3 alone, in the process 'devastating the hearts and souls of [the US] work force,' notes one observer.[65]

Not surprisingly, US corporations have lost even more ground to countries with superior management systems. Thus, while business sector productivity during the 1980s grew by an average of 3 per cent in Japan and 1.6 per cent in Germany, it rose by a mere 0.5 per cent a year in the United States.[66] The few bright spots in the US picture were the handful of firms which borrowed the Japanese method of considering layoffs only as a last resort. At General Motors' NUMMI joint venture with Toyota and at GM's Saturn plant, productivity has soared.[67]

The advent of the Clinton administration did not promise much change. For while President Clinton and his 'New Democrats' have talked about the importance of more civilian R&D, more spending on capital equipment and infrastructure, a more activist government role in strategic industrial planning, and more worker retraining, they have been silent on the question of any fundamental changes in the relationship between labor and management. Indeed, the administration's endorsement of NAFTA implies backing for US corporate capital's strategic choice of competing by relying on cheap labor.

US Capital and Global Adjustment

The 1980s, then, saw a process of corporate-driven global adjustment, which encompassed the US economy. Ideologically trumpeting the free market but in practice advancing the interest of corporate monopolies, the Reagan and Bush administrations presided over the dismantling of the New Deal state, the depression of living standards, and the destruction of workers' protections. Reaganomics was, in part, an expression of US corporate capital's drive to be liberated from the restraints imposed by big government and big labor in order to compete against the challenges to its global hegemony posed by the Third World, the NICs, and its competitors among the advanced countries, in particular Japan. There was, indeed, a strategic coherence to the adjustment that corporate capital pushed on the US, the Third World, the NICs, and Japan, and this was its fervent anti-statist thrust. US corporate strategy sought the elimination of state support of production among its competitors and potential competitors and liberation from state restraints on corporate activity in the home economy. Structural adjustment, liberalization, privatization, deregulation – these were the key thrusts of corporate America's effort to create a global playing field whose rules would favor its version of capitalism and hobble the opposition's.

However, there was a critical weakness in the US strategy. This was the US corporations' preferred mode of regaining competitiveness, which was not by investing more in infrastructure, capital equipment, research and development, and human capital, but by reasserting management's unrestricted control, depressing domestic wages and downsizing the domestic workforce, and transferring manufacturing operations to low-wage countries. Not only was this creating tremendous stresses and strains in society, it was also proving to be wholly inadequate in delivering competitiveness to the less confrontational labor–management strategies that drove the rise in productivity in Japan and Germany.

10
Dark Victory

We meant to change a nation, and instead we changed a world.

—Ronald Reagan, January 11, 1989, quoted in Lou Cannon,
President Reagan: the Role of a Lifetime (New York: Simon and
Schuster, 1991)

If the people in the emerging spheres of prosperity knew how to
think in the long term, they would watch carefully the peripheries
at their doors. In the coming world order, there will be winners
and there will be losers. The losers will outnumber the winners by
an unimaginable factor.

—Jacques Attali, *Millenium: Winners and Losers in the Coming
World Order* (New York: Random House, 1991)

[W]e need to ensure that military superiority – particularly technological superiority – remains with nations (above all the United
States) which can be trusted with it. We must never leave the
sanction of force to those who have no scruples about its use.

—Margaret Thatcher, quoted in *The Nation*
(Bangkok) Sept. 7, 1993

Corporate-driven structural adjustment triggered severe social stresses
and strains in both the North and the South. In the United States,
the Reagan and Bush administrations, having dismantled many of
the stabilizing social mechanisms of the New Deal state, could not
address the discontent and disaffection unleashed by their policies
except through largely punitive measures. US expenditures on
criminal justice increased four times faster than the budget for
education, and twice as fast as outlays on health and hospitals.[1] With
the number of Americans behind bars tripling between 1970 and 1990,
the US achieved the distinction of imprisoning a larger share of its
population than any other nation.[2]

By and large, the North's response to growing misery, anger, and strife in the South was also largely punitive in character. This was not surprising, given the Reagan–Bush era's abandonment of liberal foreign aid policies which had been designed to defuse discontent among certain sections of Third World populations. Indeed, out of fear of the consequences of adjustment policies, brazenly draconian responses began to gain a measure of popularity among Northern elites and, more ominously, among the Northern masses.

For instance, Garrett Hardin's 'lifeboat ethics,' first floated in the 1970s, began to make a comeback in the 1990s. Seeking a rollback of Third World populations out of a seeming concern for the global environment, biomedical ethicist Joseph Fletcher, a Hardin disciple, argued that famine relief should be withheld from places like the Horn of Africa, 'when it can be foreseen that the recipients will thereby live on to reproductive years and thus increase the number of starving people, plus the predictable diseases that go with starvation, because

Dresden, former East Germany, 1992. Neo-Nazis are on the rise and torching Turkish guest workers and their families. (Teit Hornmak, Impact Visuals)

their country has exceeded its carrying capacity.'[3] Development aid, Fletcher added, 'should be offered on condition that contraceptives and vasectomies "go with the groceries."' [4]

Shutting out the South

As the Northern countries themselves were subjected to harsh adjustment by corporate capital, people fleeing the devastation of the South to seek economic opportunities in the North triggered mass anxieties that were readily exploited by right-wing ideologues seeking scapegoats, or by politicians attempting to deflect public attention from the structural causes of record unemployment and deepening inequalities. In 1992, for instance, socialist French Prime Minister Edith Cresson proposed chartering planes to haul unwanted immigrants back to their home countries. Her hardline position on immigration was virtually indistinguishable from that of Giscard d'Estaing of the center-right opposition and Jean-Marie Le Pen of the racist National Front. It should therefore come as no surprise that after the conservatives came to power in France in 1993 racism and ethnocentrism were enshrined, with significant popular support, in bills adopted by the French Parliament which sought to achieve 'zero immigration.' The measures proposed included eliminating the automatic assumption of French nationality by children of immigrants born in the country, and allowing police identity checks based on one's race.

In Germany, the dangerous interplay between political opportunism and popular anxieties not only resulted in the weakening of the unconditional right of asylum adopted during the de-Nazification era, it also gave the green light to neo-Nazi groups to mount murderous attacks on foreigners, including long-time Turkish resident guestworkers. Most Germans, noted *The Economist*, 'tend to agree with the slogan "the boat is full," meaning Germany has too many foreigners. Nor do they always distinguish Turks who have been in Germany for a long time from recent "economic migrants."'[5]

In the United States, coded racist and chauvinist rhetoric by the Republicans and the far right inflamed anti-immigrant sentiment, which was given respectability by the anti-immigration platform adopted by some key environmental groups ostensibly seeking to stabilize the population at sustainable levels.

Throughout the North, liberals and social democrats retreated in disarray in the face of the anti-immigrant, anti-South mood. Indeed, intellectual and moral capitulation was the rule. For example, in his book *Millenium*, Jacques Attali, the well-known French socialist who served as the first chairman of the European Bank for Reconstruction and Development, writes off the billions of people in the South as 'millenial losers.' Africa is a 'lost continent,' while Latin America is sliding into 'terminal poverty.'[6] With no future of their own, says Attali, the peoples of the South can only look forward to 'migrating from place to place looking for a few drops of what we have in Los Angeles, Berlin, or Paris, which for them will be oases of hope, emerald cities of plenty and high-tech magic.'[7]

What worries Attali is that the poor of the South 'will redefine hope in fundamentalist terms altogether outside modernity. This dynamic threatens true world war of a new type ... terrorism that can suddenly rip the vulnerable fabric of complex systems.'[8] One possible denouement of the North–South conflict, says Attali, is a 'war unlike any other seen in modern times, [one that] will resemble the barbarian raids of the seventh and eighth centuries.'[9]

Immigrants from the South were clearly the people that Attali regarded as the barbarian raiders. For many of Attali's more reactionary compatriots, the barbarians took the form of Arab migrants from the impoverished Muslim North African countries; indeed, the barbarians were already within the gates in the shape of a large Muslim resident community, which formed a significant portion of the 4.5 million foreigners living in France. As one report saw it, 'to most French people, the word "immigré" means Turks, black Africans, Asians, and, most of all Arabs from Algeria, Morocco or Tunisia, former French colonies.'[10] And according to one experienced observer, 'many French are reacting specifically against the spread of Islam in the country.'[11]

Protracted War

Attali's image of protracted war with the South is strikingly similar to the one outlined in 1988 by the US Presidential Commission on Long-Term Strategy's *Discriminate Deterrence*, the landmark document which began the process of moving the US defense establishment's focus away from the Soviet Union toward the threat that was seen as emanating from the Third World. Struggle with the Third World, warned the Commission, would take the form of 'low-intensity conflict' – 'a form of warfare in which "the enemy" is more or less omnipresent and unlikely ever to surrender.' It went on to say that 'whereas in the past we have sometimes seen these attacks as a succession of transient and isolated crises, we now have to think of them as a permanent addition to the menu of defense planning problems.'[12]

Regarding the South as the principal enemy has since been institutionalized in US defense planning. In what was billed as the first detailed military planning for the post-Cold War era, the Pentagon in the early 1990s prepared seven scenarios of conflict – five of which saw US troops intervening in Third World countries.[13] And when the first post-Cold War intervention did take place, against Iraq in 1991, the strategic purpose, to use the euphemistic language of *The Economist*, was not to allow 'medium-sized regional powers ... to imagine that in the new [post-Cold War] environment they could rampage unchecked.'[14]

The 'Islamic Threat'

Saddam Hussein was perhaps the leading candidate among those who could be demonized into the new enemy, but by the end of the Bush administration in 1992 the single most worrisome trend for US policymakers in key parts of the Third World was said to be the 'march of Islamic fundamentalism.'[15] Like the French, many American establishment intellectuals began to talk about civilizational and cultural conflicts supplanting Cold War and class struggles, and their concerns about Islam were clearly uppermost. In one influential view, that of Harvard political scientist Samuel Huntington, the most likely prospect for conflict will be between the West and the 'Islamic-Confucian Connection'.[16] The distance separating this view from a policy of intervention in support of corrupt regimes threatened by fundamentalist Islamic movements was dangerously narrow, leading one otherwise conservative western publication to warn:

> There is now a growing danger of the West falling into the dreary cold-war trap of keeping tinpot dictators in power because of the service they do in keeping undesirables down ... To help them, for no other reason than the actual or potential threat of an Islamic uprising, is bad politics, and bad morals too.[17]

That Islamic fundamentalism was singled out by the West as the greatest potential threat to the new world order was not surprising. For, while it certainly had dismaying reactionary aspects, such as its treatment of women and its disdain for political pluralism, Islamic fundamentalism also represented a revolt against the materialism associated with Western culture, against the domination of transnational capital, and, in countries like Egypt, Tunisia, and Morocco, against the miseries imposed by IMF–World Bank structural adjustment programs. With the deep crisis of progressive secular alternatives provoked by the collapse of socialism in the Soviet Union and Eastern Europe, millions of people throughout the Third World were turning to Islamic revivalism and other forms of fundamentalism out of a yearning for community, for a holistic existence which many felt had been destroyed by capitalism's glorification of the pursuit of profits. It was this desire for human relationships which were not dominated by the profit-and-loss sheet that Attali caricatured, with both disdain and fear, as a redefinition of 'hope in fundamentalist terms outside the framework of modernity altogether.'[18]

Heading off Disaster

In sum, by the end of the Republican era, the policy of the United States and many of its key allies toward the South had evolved three principal thrusts: support for continuing structural adjustment of the economy, prevention or reduction of immigration, and periodic military expeditions to keep threatening Southern actors, like Saddam Hussein, off balance. A fourth prong was also being actively discussed: diplomatic support or active intervention in support of regimes threatened by Islamic movements.

Despite hopes to the contrary, the new Clinton administration did not evolve a different policy. Indeed, the Clinton-ordered missile strike against Baghdad in June 1993 to 'punish' Saddam for allegedly organizing an attempted assassination of former President George Bush was a deafening message to the South that adherence to the Third World policy in place was the order of the day.

Thus, the new crowd in Washington could not be relied on to arrest the deadly dynamic of polarization between two phenomena that fed off one another, fundamentalism in the South and chauvinism in the North. To disrupt this fatal relationship will require eliminating its central cause, which is the restructuring of the world economy to consolidate the hegemony of Northern, and specifically US, corporate capital. It will mean appealing to and promoting the common interests of the peoples of the North and the peoples of the South in repelling corporate-driven structural adjustment. It will entail forging, across borders, another, alternative economic vision, one that brings the economy back under the control of the community instead of having the economy drive and rend the community, one that fosters solidarity instead of the atomized existence idealized by market ideology.

There were organizations and communities throughout both the North and the South that by the beginning of the 1990s were moving toward such a vision, toward communication with one another, and toward alliance. This movement carried different banners, among them 'sustainable development' or 'people-centred development.' The question was: would it jell fast enough into a critical mass to head off the dark victory of the grim global future known as the 'new world order?'

11

The Battle for the 21st Century

The twenty-first century began with a North–South war. It will continue with a battle fought by all human kind for the collective survival of the planet. To stop this battle of all human kind for itself from turning once more into a North–South war, an alternative development is needed, in North and South ... Today, choosing peace implies choosing a new, alternative, social and ecological model.

> —Alain Lipietz, *Towards a New Economic Order:*
> *Post-Fordism, Ecology and Democracy* (New York:
> Oxford University Press, 1992)

During the carnage of the First World War, Rosa Luxemburg, the brilliant German Marxist, made her celebrated comment that Europe faced the choice of opting either for 'socialism or barbarism'.

The Faces of Barbarism

The world is confronted with a not dissimilar situation today. Barbarism stares us in the face in many guises – in clean-shaven techno-warriors who manage, from Washington, the death of hundreds of thousands in Middle Eastern battlefields that they experience as sanitized digital images in electronic monitors; in Christian Serbs who rape Muslim women *en masse* and depopulate Muslim villages in the name of 'ethnic cleansing'; in neo-Nazi German Youth who burn down the homes of Turkish guest laborers; in French rightists who advocate mass deportation of undocumented Third World workers to preserve the 'purity' of French culture; in American fundamentalists who have declared moral and cultural war on blacks, Third World immigrants, the women's movement, and liberals in their pursuit of a mythical white Christian America.

But what about the other side of Luxemburg's equation – socialism? For the era following the world wars, Luxemburg was only partially right, since it was Keynesian capitalism in either its liberal, New Deal version or its social democratic face that triumphed over fascism and proved to be more attractive to the masses than centralist socialism.

It is this reformed capitalism that is today in crisis in the North – and its crisis is paralleled by the unravelling of Third World economies in which the state has also played a critical role in promoting economic growth or forging a *modus vivendi* on the distribution of income and wealth.

No Room for Nostalgia

Clearly, in the Third World, there is no question of reverting to the state-led or state-assisted capitalism of the post-war period. For while this system did promote growth and a measure of sovereignty, it was also accompanied by the worsening of income distribution and serious environmental damage. The currently fashionable nostalgia among some Third World economists for *les trente glorieuses* (three glorious decades, 1950–1980) of state-led import-substitution indus-trialization must not be allowed to obscure its mixed record.

And there is absolutely no question, in both the North and the South, of adopting the bureaucratic socialism that reigned in Eastern Europe and the Soviet Union and is on its last legs in North Korea, China, Vietnam and Cuba. The fall of bureaucratic socialism has been a chastening experience for progressives. It has, among other things, forced them to discard the Rousseauean faith in the perfectibility of men and women given the appropriate social and economic organ-ization. It has underlined the critical link between the organization of production, efficiency and technological innovation. It has made progressives more conscious of the limits of the state as an agent of economic transformation.

Checking Capitalism's Logic

And yet, in a deeper sense, Luxemburg's conviction that socialism is the only alternative to barbarism has a distinctively contemporary relevance. It is fashionable these days to describe the desired alter-natives as an equitable, democratic, and ecologically sustainable social and economic organization. But once one begins to attempt to spell out the concrete implications of this abstract ideal, one cannot avoid describing a system of social relations that checks or restrains the devastating logic of capitalism – at least, capitalism in its Anglo-American, free-market version – to sacrifice individual well-being, community, the environment, and even the long-term viability of the economy itself on the altar of short-term profitability.

Whether one calls the alternative socialism, social democracy, democratic capitalism, or people-centered development is less important than its essence: the subordination of the market, of the institutions of production and distribution to community. The re-integration of the economy into the community cannot be left to the invisible hand of the market, for that hand constantly erodes communal bonds and makes individual insecurity the human condition. Moreover, while seemingly blind, the market is actually skewed in favor of the groups with significant assets. Neither can this reintegration be imposed from above, by coercive state power. This was the mistake common to both Stalinist socialism and Korean-style command capitalism: coercive integration and coherence is ultimately skin-deep and is thrown off by people at the first opportunity.

Cooperation and Competition

Ultimately, the reintegration of economy into community, if it is to be lasting and healthy, must derive from the conscious decision making, in democratic fashion, of the community or civil society. Whatever one wishes to call it, conscious cooperative organization must supplant both blind competition and monopolistic collusion as the strategic principle of production and exchange if the economy is to be brought back to its appropriate relationship to the community.

Such a system need not mean the end of competition, only its sub-ordination to the strategic organizing principles of cooperation equity and sustainability. Indeed, in this post-Keynesian, post-Stalinist, post-Reaganomic world, the challenge to economic innovators is how to marry capitalism's unsurpassed ability to promote productive efficiency and technological innovation to the traditional socialist movement's concern for equity and the Green Movement's demand for a New Deal between nature and society. Flexibility and principled compromise are the order of the day, not the dogmatism that unravelled both Stalinist socialism and Reaganism as credible alternatives to the Keynesian *modus vivendi*.

Internationalizing Cooperative Organization

Institutions of economic cooperation at the level of the enterprise, community, and nation need to be paralleled by mechanisms of coop-erative organization at the international level. For a key flaw of the Keynesian or 'Fordist' compromise was that while it was able to set up functioning equilibrating macroeconomic mechanisms at the national level, it was unable to institutionalize them successfully at the international level. As Alain Lipietz has pointed out, with the advent of global markets and globalized production, the chronic 'demand-side' crises that had been resolved at the national level by government spending and wage increases were transferred to the international level, and here '[t]here was of course, no multinational agreement to balance growth in different countries, no supranational welfare state, no international treaty on working hours.'[1]

What ostensibly Keynesian mechanisms were set up in the postwar period – the World Bank, International Monetary Fund, and the regional development banks – were extremely limited in their equilibrating and redistributive impacts and were, for the most part, hijacked to promote the interests of the North, particularly the United States.

The Role of Working-Class Solidarity

The basis for a new international regulatory framework has been created by the very globalization of production that undermined the Keynesian national economy. For this harsh process has brought home to workers in both North and South their common condition as workers, their common subjugation to the capitalist calculus of short-term profitability. The extreme international mobility of corporate capital coupled with the largely self-imposed national limits on labor organizing by the Northern labor unions (except when this served Washington's Cold War political objectives) was a deadly formula that brought organized labor to its knees as corporate capital, virtually unopposed, transferred manufacturing jobs from the North to cheap-labor sites in the Third World.

Organized labor in the North has been chastened by this experience, at the same time that the new, insurgent working classes in the NICs and the Third World have begun to realize the critical role of international solidarity in countering the alliance between multinational capital and local elites. Of course, chauvinist myopia continues to afflict many in the northern labor leadership, but there are signs of growing internationalist consciousness in the rank and file. Perhaps what was wrong with socialist expectations about the emergence of international labor solidarity was not that they were misplaced but that they were premature.

The Struggle for the Future

These glimmers of hope on the labor front must be seen in the context of the very rewarding experiences in transborder organizing that have occurred in the battlegrounds of human rights, peace, and the environment in the last two decades.[2] True, the victories in these areas have been limited, but they nevertheless attest to the power of the conviction that human rights, peace, and environmental welfare are indivisible and transcend the boundaries set by states – limits supported by corporate capital in the name of 'national sovereignty' when it suits its objectives.

It is the universalizing logic of labor solidarity, community, equity, and ecological sustainability that confronts the increasingly destructive combination of corporate expansionism, political counter-revolution, and tribal retrogression in the North. While the former still has to attain a critical mass, it is by no means preordained that the future belongs to the latter.

12

Epilogue: the Asian Economic Implosion

In July 1997, nine years after the biggest surprise of the twentieth century, the collapse of socialism, came its second biggest surprise: the implosion of the Asian 'tiger economies' that had been regarded almost universally as the 'engine' of the world economy in the first decades of the twenty-first century.

The Asian financial crisis is now well into its second year, and there is no relief in sight. Indeed, a brief survey of the social scene reveals an almost universally depressing landscape, though there are some optimistic vignettes here and there.

- What Koreans call 'IMF suicides' are said to be on the increase in Seoul these days. This phenomenon refers to males who are laid off, taking not only their own lives but also those of their wives and children, presumably out of a belief that no one will be left to care for them.
- In 1998, Thais woke up to television images of workers battling police in the streets, then being herded prisoner-of-war style into police vans. Viewers thought the scenes were from Korea and were surprised to learn that they were from Thailand, a country well known for its non-confrontative culture.
- In Indonesia, the economy is expected to contract by 15 to 25 per cent by the end of 1998, but there is a silver lining to this tragedy: the government's decision to implement an IMF directive to end energy subsidies in May 1998 provoked a mass uprising that overthrew the 32-year-old Suharto dictatorship.

Welcome to Asia 1999 – a zone of economic collapse, social crisis, IMF suzerainty, and political turbulence.

Living through current events, one experiences a time warp, a throwback to 1968, when East Asia was the world's prime crisis area. It is hard to imagine that this is the same region that was being touted as recently as 15 months ago as the 'engine of the world economy' far into the twenty-first century. I think it is fair to say that the East Asian implosion is probably the second biggest surprise of the twentieth century after the collapse of the economies of Eastern Europe.

What happened? Why were Asia's tiger economies so fragile, after all?

The Collapse

In recent months, 'crony capitalism' has become the all-purpose explanation for the Asian economic collapse. Lack of transparency of financial institutions, a government-business relationship permeated with corruption, and the absence of accountability of political and economic authorities are said to be the practices that brought the Asian tigers to their knees.

The problem with this explanation is that the practices of 'crony capitalism' were very much part of economic life in the three decades that East Asian countries led the world in GNP growth. Crony capitalism has become so elastic in its connotations – which range from corruption to any kind of government activism in economic policymaking – as to become useless as an explanatory construct. It is one thing to say that corruption has pervaded relations between government and business in East Asia, as it has in Italy or the United States, where it is legalized through such mechanisms as 'political action committees' (PACs) that make support of politicians contingent on promises of favorable treatment of corporate interests. It is quite another thing to say that corruption is the principal reason for the downfall of the East Asian economies.

Though the *Wall Street Journal* and *The Economist* regularly pronounce crony capitalism to be the villain of the piece, many financial insiders in Asia find the thesis ridiculous. Perhaps the matter is best put in perspective by Kenneth Courtis, chief economist for the Deutsche Bank Group Asia Pacific:

> We have been told for a year that this crisis is the result of some politicians in Bangkok who got their hands caught in the cookie jar. Can you believe for a moment that a country that has a GNP a third of the capitalization of General Electric could all of a sudden – as if it never had corrupt politicians before – get things wrong and set off a global, systemic, virulent financial crisis that's shaking markets around the world?[1]

While not denying that corruption may have been an accessory to the collapse, many serious analysts have come around to the view that a far greater role was played by the unregulated flows of global capital. Like the Mexican financial collapse of 1994, the Asian crisis is essentially a product of the globalization of financial markets. Or as Courtis, using the financial analyst's jargon, puts it: 'This crisis is not an Asian crisis. It's a global emerging market crisis.'[2]

A close look at the rise and fall of the Southeast Asian 'tigers' reveals the central role of a development process sustained not principally by domestic savings and investment but by the huge infusions of foreign capital. In the late 1980s, the region's growth was heavily dependent on Japanese direct investment. When this began to taper off in the early 1990s, the region's financial and technocrat elites sought other sources of foreign capital. These they found in the portfolio investors and big international banks that were scouring the globe at around the same time in search of alternatives to the low real interest rates and declining returns in the stock markets of New York, London, and Tokyo.

Mediating the relationship between the banks and investors and what came to be fashionably termed the 'big emerging markets' was the International Monetary Fund (IMF), which pushed the Asian financial authorities incessantly to liberalize their capital account and open their financial sector more fully to foreign participation. With the blessings of the Fund, the authorities added two more ingredients: high interest rates and a fixed rate of exchange between the local currency and the dollar to insure investors against the risk of devaluations that could erode the value of their investments.

This formula was wildly successful in bringing in capital: according to Washington's Institute of International Finance, net private capital flows to Indonesia, Malaysia, the Philippines, Thailand, and Korea shot up from $37.9 billion in 1994 to $79.2 billion in 1995 to $97.1 billion in 1996.[3]

However, there were two fundamental problems with this strategy, which came together in harrowing fashion in 1997.

First, as economists Jayati Ghosh and C.P. Chandrasekhar have pointed out, there was a basic contradiction between encouraging foreign capital inflows and keeping an exchange rate that would make one's exports competitive in world markets. The former demanded a currency pegged to the dollar at a stable rate in order to draw in foreign investors. With the dollar appreciating in 1995 and 1996, so did the pegged Southeast Asian currencies, and so did the international prices of Southeast Asian exports. This process cut deeply into the competitiveness of economies that had staked their growth on ever increasing exports.[4]

The second problem was that the bulk of the funds coming in was speculative capital seeking high and quick returns. With little regulation of its movements by governments that bought into the IMF's laissez faire ideology and that had little experience in handling such massive inflows, foreign capital gravitated, not to the productive sectors of the economy like agriculture and manufacturing but to the stock market, consumer financing, and, in particular, real estate. In Bangkok at the height of the real estate boom in the early 1990s land values were higher than in urban California!

Not surprisingly, a glut in real estate developed quite rapidly, with Bangkok leading the way with $20 billion worth of new commercial and residential space unsold by 1996. Foreign banks had competed to push loans onto Thai banks, finance companies, and enterprises in the boom years of the early 1990s. In 1996, it began to sink in that their borrowers were loaded with non-performing loans.

At the same time, alarm bells were sounded by the flat export growth rates for 1996 – an astonishing zero growth in the case of both Malaysia and Thailand – and burgeoning current account deficits. Since a foreign exchange surplus gained through consistently rising exports of goods and services was the ultimate guarantee that the massive foreign debt contracted by the private sector would be repaid, this was massive blow to investor confidence. What the investors failed to realize, however, was that the very policy of maintaining a strong currency that was calculated to draw them in was also the very cause of the export collapse. And what many also failed to realize was that the upgrading of the quality of exports that could have counteracted the rise in export prices had been undermined by the easy flow of foreign money into the speculative sectors of the economy, as manufacturers chose to channel their investments there to gain quick profits instead of pouring them into research and development and upgrading the skills of the work force.[5]

By 1997, it was time to get out, and because of the liberalization of the capital account, there were no mechanisms to slow down the exit of funds. With hundreds of billions of baht chasing a limited amount of dollars, the outflow of capital could be highly destabilizing. What converted a nervous departure into a catastrophic stampede were the currency speculators who, gambling on the eventual devaluation of the baht, in fact accelerated it by unloading huge quantities of baht in search of dollars. By July 2, 1997, the decade-long peg of the baht to the dollar at 25 baht – $1 was abandoned, and the Thai currency went on to lose over 50 per cent of its value in only a few months.

In Jakarta, Manila, and Kuala Lumpur, there occurred the same sequence of property glut, non-performing loans, foreign capital's departure turned into a panic by currency speculators, the currency crash. Southeast Asia's other currencies lost 30 to 80 per cent of their value. The scale of destabilization caused by the panic is indicated by the figures: from a net inflow of $93 billion in 1996, private capital flow into the five most troubled Asian economies turned into a net outflow of $12 billion in 1997.[6]

A Failure of Leadership

The scale, depth, and swiftness of the crisis demanded a decisive leadership to formulate and implement a comprehensive strategic response. But there has only been one government that has behaved in a regionally responsible fashion, and that is China. China contributed money to rescue funds for Thailand, Indonesia, and Korea. It offered to back the proposed Asian Monetary Fund with its reserves. And it has refrained from devaluing its currency, the renmimbi, so as not to stand in the way of an export-led recovery by its neighbors.

But, the behavior of the Chinese aside, effective leadership has been the most scarce currency in the Asian currency crisis.

Valuable time was lost when, instead of acknowledging that volatile capital flows brought about by liberalization of the capital account and financial liberalization were the fundamental cause of the crisis, Washington and the IMF insisted that 'crony capitalism', or corrupt relations between the private and public sectors, was the main issue and that the solution lay principally in eliminating corruption and achieving greater 'transparency.'

Instead of leading an effort to stabilize and reflate the region in a manner akin to the way it revived Western Europe with the Marshall Plan after World War II, Washington has, in the opinion of many, forsaken 'enlightened self interest' and opportunistically seized the chance to use the IMF to advance its bilateral agenda for the region – that is, to batter down the tariff and investment barriers to US exports and capital.

Furthermore instead of standing up to Washington and the IMF to provide an alternative economic program to shore up the regional economy, Japan failed to live up to the rest of Asia's expectations that it was prepared to take a regional leadership role when it yielded to Washington's pressure to scrap its plan to set up the $100 billion Asian Monetary Fund (AMF) that would have defended the Asian currencies from investor panic and further speculative attack.[7] Japan, in fact, has missed the boat, in the opinion of many Asians. They do not think the Japanese will ever be able to break with the psychology of the Occupation, which is now the key factor preventing it from making decisions that would reflate the region as well as respond to its self-interest, since Asia, before the crisis, was a bigger trading partner and a source of more profits from investments than the United States.

The IMF Worsens the Crisis

Instead of effective leadership, the region got the IMF.

In response to the regional collapse, the IMF assembled rescue packages totalling $120 billion for Korea, Indonesia, and Thailand. But the institution soon found itself under fire from critics in the North and South, from both progressives and conservatives.

A major criticism levelled at the Fund is that, by promoting a policy of indiscriminate capital account liberalization among the East Asian economies, it has been a central cause of the crisis. Not only is this the case, but the IMF stabilization programs continue to push radical financial liberalization, ignoring the mounting evidence that it is uncontrolled capital movements that triggered the crisis.

Critics also charge that while the bailouts are being billed as a rescue of economies, they are actually geared to providing a guarantee to the international private banks that the debt to them will be repaid by the borrowing countries. Thus the IMF rescue programs, by sparing foreign investors and banks from the penalties of the market, encourage 'moral hazard' or continued irresponsible lending in the future.

A third charge levelled against the Fund is that it is being manipulated by its principal and strongest stockholder, the United States, to push trade and investment reforms that would benefit principally US economic interests. In the case of Korea, for instance, the US Treasury Department and the IMF have not concealed their close working relationship.

Not surprisingly, the concessions made by the Koreans in the negotiation of the IMF program – including raising the limit on foreign ownership of corporate stocks to 55 per cent and full liberalization of the local capital market – have a one-to-one correspondence with Washington's bilateral economic policy toward Korea over the last decade. As the undersecretary of the US Treasury Department, Larry Summers, has candidly admitted: 'In some ways the IMF has done more in these past months to liberalize these economies and open their markets to US goods and services than has been achieved in rounds of trade negotiations in the region.'[8]

Perhaps the most powerful criticism of the IMF is that it is imposing the wrong solution on the financially devastated countries. The universal prescription of the Fund consists of the maintenance of high interest rates and significant cuts in government expenditures. Promoted as necessary to bring back foreign investors and stabilize the economy, the adjustment programs are engineering recessions. Expansionary fiscal and monetary policies, say critics like Harvard's Jeffrey Sachs, are needed to counter the collapse of private investment and prevent the economy from going into a free fall.[9] And if the intention is – as the IMF says it is – to bring back foreign investment into the country, how would this be accomplished by engineering a recession that promises little or nothing in the way of profits?

The view that IMF programs are making a bad situation worse is no longer a fringe view. It is shared by many World Bank technocrats, including reportedly the Bank's chief economist Joseph Stiglitz,[10] as well as by key members of the US Congress, who have refused so far to approve the $14.5 billion demanded by the Clinton administration to fund a US quota increase on the grounds that it would be throwing good money after bad.

The Social Costs

The resolution to this policy debate on the role of the IMF will have major consequences on the ground. In Thailand, it can no longer be denied that the depressive effects of the financial crash have been deepened by the IMF program, resulting in a change from the initial IMF estimate of a 2.5 per cent growth in gross domestic product in 1998 to the latest estimate of a negative 8 per cent growth. Similarly, the Korean economy is contracting much faster than anticipated under the Fund's stabilization program, with the IMF revising its early estimate of GDP growth in 1998 from 1 per cent to a negative 1 per cent. As for Indonesia, the most optimistic estimate is that the GNP will contract by 15 per cent in 1998, with most private analysts projecting a decline of 20–25 per cent.

These macroeconomic indicators translate into tremendous suffering on the ground. Already, 2.2 million people in Thailand – around 6 per cent of the workforce – have been thrown out of work by the combination of the financial crisis and IMF-engineered recession. With an average of 2,000 people losing their jobs everyday, total unemployment at the end of 1998 is expected to encompass four million workers, or 15 per cent of the workforce.

In Indonesia, the recently renegotiated program will certainly accelerate an economic free-fall that has already raised the number of people living under the poverty line from 22.5 million to 118.5 million, or from 11.2 per cent of the population to 60.6 per cent.

In Korea, many observers estimate that the numbers of unemployed will exceed two million by the end of 1998, or 9 per cent of the workforce. These bleak prospects will require a great deal of psychological adjustment on the part of a labor force that is accustomed to a system of lifetime employment and has little or nothing in the way of unemployment compensation.

Crisis and Opportunity?

With people throughout Asia having their backs to the wall, what is to be done?

Launching into the prescriptive mode is the most challenging – and frustrating – part of any analysis, but, as people in Bangkok say these days, current policies are so bad that any alternative would be better.

The most urgent need at the moment is to put a stop to the depressive programs of the IMF and to launch expansionary programs based on aggressive deficit spending and bringing down interest rates. While some governments, such as Thailand's, are beginning to stand up to the Fund and – with some success – pushing reflationary programs, it will take a coordinated effort among the governments of the region to effect a policy reversal.

Regional cooperation is the order of the day not only when it comes to dealing with the Fund, but on a number of pressing issues as well: macroeconomic policy, trade policy, currency stabilization, and foreign debt policy. Coordination on currency stabilization and debt repayment strategies is especially crucial.

With respect to currency stabilization, it is critical to convince Japan to defy the US and resurrect its proposal for an Asian Regional Fund that would pool together the reserves of the reserve-rich countries – Japan, China, Taiwan, Hong Kong, and Singapore – into a $100 billion war chest aimed at defending the region's currencies against the moves of speculators. On debt strategy, the East Asian economies must not repeat the experience of the 1980s, when the creditors united behind the IMF to take advantage of the disunity of the debtors to pick them off one by one and impose draconian debt repayment programs on all. The renegotiation of the debt must be done on the basis of the principle that a large part of the debt is private debt and that both private debtors and private lenders must be forced to accept the penalties imposed by the market for making the wrong decision. The burden of servicing the debt must not be pushed onto the people, which is the IMF solution. Public monies must not be used to bail out big private creditors.

On the domestic front, there must be a comprehensive strategy with short-term, medium-term, and long-term components.

The short-term must include bringing down interest rates and using currency controls to stabilize the exchange rate – a measure that even a neoclassical economist like Paul Krugman now proposes.[11] This is the easy part. More difficult are the medium- and long-term measures to set these economies on a firmer, more healthy foundation. These measures must respond to the reality that neither the free-market approach nor the dominant approach of state-assisted capitalism is an appropriate response to the crisis. Badly needed is an approach that transcends the increasingly irrelevant state vs. market dichotomy.

The key lesson of the crisis is not too much state intervention but lack of it. The rapid entry and exit of billions of dollars of speculative capital, the flow of this capital into real estate, the shifting of funds that should have gone into research and development to speculative activities, as happened with the chaebol in Korea – all these could have been prevented by a state willing to discipline the market. At the same time, state intervention geared to promoting specific private interests, as was the case in Indonesia, is not desirable either. This is not so much because it stymies growth, as the crony capitalist thesis argues, but because it promotes growth of the wrong kind, increases social inequality, and triggers environmental degradation.[12] Thus, the state must be reformed along the lines of more transparency, more accountability, and more democratic surveillance of government, but the aim of this enterprise is not to banish it as an economic agent but to enable it to more effectively regulate the market.

What is being advanced here is not just the reform of the state but the transformation of the economic regime. While market and state must continue to play a vital economic role, the fundamental mechanism of production, distribution, and exchange will have to be located elsewhere. The emerging view in many circles is that the fundamental economic mechanism must be democratic decision making by communities, civic organizations, and people's movements. The challenge is how to operationalize such institutions of economic democracy.

This movement towards economic democracy must facilitate transformations in other key dimensions of the economy along the following lines:

- Foreign investment continues to be important for development, but it must be direct foreign investment, not speculative investment. For as even Singapore's *Business Times*, a newspaper which is not exactly noted for its radical views, has noted, one of the key lessons of the crisis is that 'short-term capital inflows are of highly dubious benefit when all they do is to finance asset inflation (stocks and real estate) and a nation is arguably better off without them.'[13] Moreover, investment must be direct foreign investment of the right kind, one that contributes to improving the technological capacity of the economy, respects labor standards, and does not degrade the environment. Much of the 'growth' promoted by Asia's fast-track capitalism has really been purchased at the price of social welfare and the environment.

- While foreign investment of the right kind is important, growth must be financed principally from domestic savings and investment. This means good, progressive taxation systems. One of the key reasons for the adoption of fast-track development strategies was that the elites of East Asia did not want to tax themselves to produce the needed investment capital. Even in the depths of today's crisis, conspicuous consumption continues to mark the behavior of Asia's elites. Regressive taxation systems are the norm in the region, where income taxpayers are but a handful and indirect taxes that cut into the resources of lower-income groups are the principal source of government expenditures.

- Another major change concerns the domestic market's role in development. While export markets are important, development must be reoriented around the domestic market as the principal locomotive of growth. Together with the pitfalls of excessive reliance on foreign capital, the lessons of the crisis include the consequences of the tremendous dependence of the region's economies on export markets. This has only led to extreme vulnerability to the vagaries of the global market and sparked the current self-defeating race to 'export one's way out of the crisis' through competitive devaluation of the currency. This idea is but the latest and most desperate manifestation of the panacea of export-oriented development.

- Making the domestic market the engine of development brings up the linkage between sustained growth and equity, for a 'Keynesian' strategy of enlarging the domestic market to generate growth means increasing effective demand or bringing more consumers into the market via a comprehensive program of asset and income redistribution, including land reform. There is in this, of course, the unfinished social justice agenda of the progressive movement in Asia – an agenda that has been marginalized by the regnant ideology of growth during the miracle years.

Vast numbers of people remain marginalized because of grinding poverty, particularly in the countryside. Land and asset reform would simultaneously bring them into the market, empower them economically and politically, and create the conditions for social and political stability. Achieving economic sustainability based on a dynamic domestic market can no longer be divorced from issues of equity.

• While there are other elements in the alternative development thinking taking place in the region, one universal theme is 'sustainable development.' The centrality of ecological sustainability is said to be one of the hard lessons of the crisis. For the model of foreign capital-fueled high-speed growth is leaving behind little that is of positive value and much that is negative. In the case of Thailand, at least, it is hard to dispute this contention by the reformers. As any visitor to Bangkok these days would testify, 12 years of fast-track capitalism is leaving behind few traces except industrial plant that will be antiquated in a few years, hundreds of unoccupied high-rises, a horrendous traffic problem that is only slightly mitigated by the repossession of thousands of late-model cars from bankrupt owners, a rapid rundown of the country's natural capital, and an environment that has been irreversibly, if not mortally impaired, to the detriment of future generations.

In place of 8-10 per cent growth rates, many environmentalists in the region are now talking of rates of 3 to 4 per cent, or even lower. This links the social agenda with the environmental agenda, for one reason for the push for high growth rates was so that the elites could corner a significant part of economic growth while still allowing some growth to trickle down to the lower classes for the sake of social peace. The alternative – redistribution of wealth – is clearly less acceptable to the ruling groups, but it is the key to a pattern of development that combines economic growth, political stability, and ecological sustainability.

Articulating these ideas in this manner makes the process appear like one that will be won on rationality. Would that this were the case! In fact, these ideas and other progressive proposals remain to be welded together into a coherent strategy, and that strategy in turn awaits a mass movement to carry it. The emergence of such a movement must not be underestimated. One clear lesson of the crisis is that the region's elites are anachronistic. They will fight their displacement, as Suharto did, but the drastic loss of legitimacy stemming from their economic mismanagement provides a window of opportunity for progressive movements, like Thailand's Forum of the Poor – a unique alliance of environmentalists, farmers, and workers – to translate their ideas into effective political strategies for change. Frozen during the years of the long boom, mass politics with a class edge is about to return to center stage.

Notes and References

Chapter 1: Introduction: The Great Reversal

1. See Chapter 6 for more statistics and a fuller discussion on trends in income, poverty, and inequality in the South.
2. See Chakravarthi Raghavan, *Recolonization: GATT, the Uruguay Round, and the Third World* (Penang: Third World Network, 1990).
3. See Chapter 9 for more statistics and analysis of trends in poverty, inequality, and income in the United States.

Chapter 2: Challenge from the South

1. KPMG, *The Asia-Pacific Region: Economic and Business Prospects* (Amsterdam: KPMG, 1988), p. 4.
2. South Commission, *The Challenge to the South* (New York: Oxford University Press, 1990), p. 32.
3. Ibid.
4. John Sheahan, 'Development Dichotomies and Economic Strategy,' in Simon Teitel, ed., *Toward a New Development Strategy for Latin America* (Washington, DC: Inter-American Development Bank, 1992), p. 37.
5. South Commission, p. 32.
6. Ibid., p. 33.
7. Karin Lissakers, *Banks, Borrowers, and the Establishment: a Revisionist Account of the International Debt Crisis* (New York: Basic Books, 1991), p. 69.
8. Pedro Gerchunoff and Juan Carlos Torre, 'What Role for the State in Latin America?,' in Teitel, ed., *Toward a New Development Strategy for Latin America*, p. 262.

Chapter 3: Liberalism and Containment

1. Jerry Sanders, *Peddlers of Crisis: The Committee on the Present Danger and the Politics of Containment* (London: Pluto Press, 1983).
2. Roger Stone, *The Nature of Development: a Report from the Rural Tropics on the Quest for Sustainable Economic Growth* (New York: Alfred Knopf, 1992), p. 39.
3. Quoted in Bernard Nossiter, *The Global Struggle for More* (New York: Harper and Row, 1987), p. 35.
4. Ibid., pp. 34–5.
5. On protectionism and foreign investment regulation in Korea and Taiwan, see Chapter 8. See also Walden Bello and Stephanie Rosenfeld,

Dragons in Distress: Asia's Miracle Economies in Crisis (London: Penguin Books, 1991), pp. 47–61, 231–277.

6. Stone, p. 37.
7. Quoted in Nossiter, p. 117.
8. Patrick Lloyd Hatcher, *The Suicide of an Elite: American Internationalists and Vietnam* (Stanford, Calif.: Stanford University Press, 1990), pp. 19–20.
9. Deborah Shapley, *Promise and Power: the Life and Times of Robert McNamara* (Boston, Mass.: Little, Brown, 1993), p. 546.
10. Ibid., p. 510.
11. World Bank, AEADB Division, 'Philippine Country Program Paper,' March 26, 1976, pp. 2, 17. See also Walden Bello et al., *Development Debacle: the World Bank in the Philippines* (San Francisco: Food First, 1982).
12. Quoted in Karin Lissakers, *Banks, Borrowers and the Establishment: a Revisionist Account of the International Debt Crisis* (New York: Basic Books, 1991), p. 112.
13. Ibid., pp. 52–3.
14. Ibid., p. 53.
15. Ibid., p. 56.
16. Eduardo White, 'The Question of Foreign Investments and the Economic Crisis of Latin America,' in Richard Feinberg and Ricardo Ffrench-Davis, (eds), *Development and External Debt in Latin America: Bases for a New Consensus* (Notre Dame, Ind.: University of Notre Dame Press, 1988), pp. 157–8.
17. Lissakers, p. 56.
18. White, p. 158.

Chapter 4: Reaganism and Rollback

1. One of the best elucidations of Rollback Republicanism is provided by Franz Schurmann in his *The Logic of World Power* (New York: Pantheon Books, 1974), pp. 161–72.
2. Doug Bandow, 'The US Role in Promoting Third World Development,' in Heritage Foundation, *US Aid to the Developing World: a Free Market Agenda* (Washington, DC: Heritage Foundation, 1985), p. xxiii.
3. Ibid.
4. Ibid.
5. Ibid., pp. xxiii–xxiv.
6. Ibid., p. xxiv.
7. Ibid.
8. Ibid., p. 60.
9. Peter Bauer and Basil Yamey, 'Foreign Aid: What is at Stake?,' *The Public Interest*, Summer 1982, p. 60.
10. Ibid., p. 57.
11. Ibid., p. 54.
12. Karin Lissakers, *Banks, Borrowers and the Establishment: a Revisionist Account of the International Debt Crisis* (New York: Basic Books, 1991), p. 32.

13. Altaf Gauhar, 'Arab Petrodollars,' *World Policy Journal,* Vol. 4, No. 3 (Summer 1987), p. 463.
14. Robert Walgate, *Miracle or Menace: Biotechnology and the Third World* (London: Panos Institute, 1990), pp. 61–2.
15. Quoted in Bernard Nossiter, *The Global Struggle for More* (New York: Harper and Row, 1987), p. 6.
16. Frances Moore Lappé, Rachel Schurman, and Kevin Danaher, *Betraying the National Interest* (New York: Grove Press, 1987), p. 10.
17. Bandow, p. xxviii. See also Mark Huber, 'Humanitarian Aid,' in Heritage Foundation, pp. 1–11.
18. William Peterson, 'The Social Roots of Hunger and Overpopulation,' *The Public Interest,* Summer 1982, p. 68.
19. A.W. Clausen, quoted in Joyce Kolko, *Restructuring the World Economy* (New York: Pantheon, 1988), p. 272.
20. Morris Miller, *Coping is Not Enough!: the International Debt Crisis and the Roles of the World Bank and International Monetary Fund* (Homewood, Ill.: Dow Jones Irwin, 1986), pp. 185–6.
21. John Sheahan, 'Development Dichotomies and Economic Strategy,' in Simon Teitel, ed., *Towards a New Development Strategy for Latin America* (Washington, DC: Inter-American Development Bank, 1992), p. 33.
22. Quoted in Morris Miller, *Debt and the Environment: Converging Crises* (New York: United Nations Publications, 1991), p. 215.
23. Lissakers, pp. 228–9.
24. Ibid., p. 229.
25. Sheahan, p. 33.
26. World Bank, 'Third Report on Adjustment Lending: Private and Public Resources for Growth,' World Bank, Washington, DC, March 1992, pp. 74–6.
27. Cited in Seamus Cleary, 'Towards a New Adjustment in Africa,' in 'Beyond Adjustment,' special issue of *African Environment,* Vol. 7, Nos 1–4 (1990), p. 357.
28. Pedro Gerchunoff and Juan Carlos Torre, 'What Role for the State in Latin America?,' in Simon Teitel, ed., *Towards a New Development Strategy for Latin America,* p. 276.

Chapter 5: Adjustment: the Record

1. World Bank, *Global Economic Prospects and the Developing Countries 1993* (Washington, DC: World Bank, 1993), back cover.
2. Mohsin Khan, 'The Macroeconomic Effects of Fund-Supported Adjustment Programs,' *International Monetary Fund Staff Papers,* Vol. 37, No. 2 (June 1990), p. 215.
3. Mohsin Khan, quoted in Peter Robinson and Somsak Tambunlertchai, 'Africa and Asia: Can High Rates of Economic Growth Be Replicated?,' *Occasional Papers,* International Center for Economic Growth, No. 40 (1993), p. 24.
4. Eva Jespersen, 'External Shocks, Adjustment Policies, and Social Performance,' in Giovanni Andrea Cornia *et. al.,* eds., *Africa's Recovery*

in the 1990s: from Stagnation to Human Development (New York: St Martins Press, 1992), p. 15.
5. Ibid.
6. Ibid.
7. Frances Stewart, 'Short-Term Policies for Long-Term Development,' in Cornia et al., p. 332.
8. Jose Maria Fanelli, Roberto Frenkel, and Lance Taylor, 'The World Development Report 1991: a Critical Assessment,' in *International Monetary and Financial Issues for the 1990s* (New York: United Nations Conference on Trade and Development, 1992).
9. Ibid., p. 3.
10. Ibid.
11. Ibid., p. 15.
12. Richard Cronin, Congressional Research Service, 'Prepared Statement before Joint Committee Hearing on Japan and the Asia-Pacific Region,' July 22, 1992, p. 3.
13. Djisman Simandjuntak, 'Indonesia's Marathon of Economic Reform: on the Strong Road to a Market Economy,' in David Timberman, ed., *The Politics of Economic Reform in Southeast Asia* (Manila: Asian Institute of Management, 1992), p. 56.
14. Chaipat Sakasakul, *Lessons from the World Bank's Experience of Structural Adjustment Loans (SALs): a Case Study of Thailand* (Bangkok: Thailand Development Research Institute, 1992), p. 19; and Narongchai Akrasanee, David Dapice, Frank Flatters, *Thailand's Export Led Growth: Retrospect and Prospects* (Bangkok: Thailand Development Research Institute, 1991), p. 17.
15. Thailand Development Research Institute (TDRI), *Thailand's Economic Structure*: Summary Report (Bangkok: TDRI, 1992), pp. 2, 26
16. Fanelli, Frenkel, and Taylor, p. 19.
17. Michael Carter and Christopher Barrett, 'Does It Take More than Liberalization? The Economics of Sustainable Agrarian Growth and Transformation,' draft, University of Wisconsin, Madison, Wisconsin, April 15, 1993, pp. 10–12.
18. Fanelli, Frenkel, and Taylor, p. 14.
19. Rudiger Dornbusch, quoted in Jacques Polak, 'The Changing Nature of IMF Conditionality,' *Essays in International Finance*, Princeton University, No. 184 (September 1991), p. 47.
20. An insightful discussion of this vicious cycle is found in Robinson and Tambunlertchai, pp. 24–7.
21. Karin Lissakers, *Banks, Borrowers, and the Establishment: a Revisionist Account of the International Debt Crisis* (New York: Basic Books, 1991), pp. 242–3.
22. Morris Miller, *Debt and the Environment: Converging Crises* (New York: United Nations, 1991), p. 215.
23. Rudiger Dornbusch and Steven Marcus, 'Introduction,' in Dornbusch and Marcus, eds, *International Money and Debt* (San Francisco: International Center for Economic Growth, 1991), p. 13.

132   *Dark Victory*

24. Damian Fraser, 'Mexico Turns to Import Curbs as Deficit Grows,' *Financial Times*, April 28, 1993.
25. Dornbusch and Marcus, p. 11.
26. Ricardo Grinspun and Maxwell Cameron, 'Mexico: the Wages of Trade,' *Report on the Americas*, Vol. XXVI, No. 4 (February 1993), p. 34.
27. Ibid., p. 35.
28. Ibid.
29. Inter-American Development Bank, *Economic and Social Progress in Latin America 1991* (Washington, DC: Inter-American Development Bank, 1991), p. 124.
30. Inter-American Development Bank, *Economic and Social Progress in Latin America 1992* (Washington, DC: International Development Bank, 1992), p. 134.
31. Grinspun and Cameron, p. 37.
32. Ben Petrazzini, 'Foreign Direct Investment in Latin America's Privatization,' in Paul Boeker, ed., *Latin America's Turnaround: Privatization, Foreign Investment, and Growth* (International Center for Economic Growth and the Institute for the Americas, 1993), pp. 58–60.
33. Inter-American Development Bank, *Economic and Social Progress ... 1992*, p. 134.
34. Petrazzini, pp. 61–6; 'A New Rush to Latin America,' *New York Times*, Section 3, April 11, 1993.
35. Grinspun and Cameron, p. 37.
36. Dominique Hatchette and Rolf Luders, 'Chile,' in Boeker, ed., pp. 22–3.
37. Alvaro Diaz, *El capitalismo chileno en los 90: crecimiento económico y desigualdad social* (Santiago: PAS, 1991), p. 58.
38. Ricardo Ffrench-Davis and Carlos Munoz, 'Economic and Political Instability in Chile,' in Simon Teitel, ed., *Towards a New Development Strategy for Latin America* (Washington, DC: Inter-American Development Bank, 1992), p. 290.
39. Inter-American Development Bank, *Economic and Social Progress ... 1992*, p. 286.
40. Fanelli, Frankel and Taylor, p. 23.
41. Ffrench-Davis and Munoz, p. 286.
42. John Sheahan, 'Development Dichotomies and Economic Strategy,' in Teitel, ed., *Towards a New Development Strategy for Latin America*, p. 30.
43. Ffrench-Davis and Munoz, p. 286; Hobart Spalding, 'Devastation in the Southern Cone: the Inheritance of the Neo-Liberal Years,' *Latin American Issues*, No. 11 (1992), p. 15.
44. Patricio Meller, *Adjustment and Equity in Chile* (Paris: OECD, 1992), pp. 61, 77.
45. Ibid., pp. 76–7.
46. Ibid., p. 77.
47. Diaz, p. 53; 'Chile Advances in a War on Poverty and One Million Mouths Say "Amen",' *New York Times*, April 4, 1993.
48. Diaz, p. 59.
49. Meller, pp. 76–7.

50. 'The Riddle of the Chairman,' *Financial Times*, August 17, 1992.
51. Jespersen, p. 12.
52. 'The Riddle of the Chairman ...'
53. Data from *World Bank Debt Tables, 1991–92* (Washington, DC: World Bank, 1991), p. 150.
54. Stewart, p. 323.
55. World Bank, *World Bank Development Report 1992: Development and the Environment* (Washington, DC: 1992), p. 244.
56. Jespersen, p. 51.
57. Charles Abugre, 'Behind the Crowded Shelves: an Assessment of Ghana's Structural Adjustment Experiences, 1983–1991,' (San Francisco: Institute for Food and Development Policy, 1993), p. 87.
58. Alice Amsden and Rolph Van der Hoeven, 'Manufacturing Output and Wages in the 1980s: Labor's Loss toward Century's End,' paper prepared for the Conference on Sustainable Development with Equity in the 1990s, Global Studies Program, University of Wisconsin, Madison, Wisconsin, May 13–16, 1993, pp. 18–19.
59. Robinson and Tambunlertchai, p. 13.
60. Abugre, p. 87.
61. Francois Bourgignon and Christian Morrison, *Adjustment and Equity in Developing Countries: a New Approach* (Paris: OECD, 1992), p. 105.
62. Ibid., p. 37.
63. Alan Roe and Hartmut Schneider, *Adjustment and Equity in Ghana* (Paris: OECD, 1992), p. 114.
64. Ibid.
65. Ibid., p. 18.
66. Stewart, p. 323.
67. Jespersen, p. 22.
68. Jeffrey Herbst, *US Economic Policy in Africa* (New York: Council on Foreign Relations Press, 1992), p. 51.
69. Abugre, p. 86.
70. United Nations Children's Fund, *The State of the World's Children 1993* (New York: Oxford University Press, 1993), p. 78.
71. Ibid.

Chapter 6: Adjustment: The Costs

1. James Gustave Spaeth, 'A Post-Rio Compact,' *Foreign Policy*, No. 88 (Fall 1992), p. 149.
2. United Nations Development Program (UNDP), *Human Development Report 1991* (New York: Oxford University Press, 1991), p. 23.
3. Ibid., p. 22.
4. Enrique Iglesias, *Reflections on Economic Development: toward a New Latin American Consensus* (Washington, DC: Inter-American Development Bank, 1992), p. 103.
5. Stephen Fidler, 'Trouble with the Neighbors,' *Financial Times*, February 16, 1993, p. 15.
6. Iglesias, p. 103.

7. Fidler, p. 15.
8. UNDP, p. 34.
9. Robin Wright and Doyle McManus, *Flashpoints: Promise and Peril in a New World* (New York: Alfred Knopf, 1991), p. 211.
10. Ibid., p. 162.
11. Richard Webb, 'Domestic Crisis and Foreign Debt in Peru,' in Richard Feinberg and Ricardo Ffrench-Davis, eds, *Development and External Debt in Latin America: Bases for a New Consensus* (Notre Dame, Ind.: Indiana University Press, 1988), p. 252.
12. Wright and McManus, p. 163.
13. Lester Thurow, *Head to Head: the Coming Struggle among Japan, Europe, and the United States* (New York: William Morrow, 1992), p. 216.
14. World Bank, *World Debt Tables, 1991–92* Vol. 1 (Washington, DC: World Bank, 1991), p. 120, 124.
15. World Bank, *Global Economic Prospects and the Developing Countries* (Washington, DC: World Bank, 1993), p. 66.
16. UNDP, p. 23.
17. Eva Jespersen, 'External Shocks, Adjustment Policies, and Economic and Social Performance,' in Giovanni Andrea Cornia et al., eds, *Africa's Recovery in the 1990s: from Stagnation to Human Development* (New York: St Martin's Press, 1992), pp. 40–1.
18. D. Muntemba, cited in Meredeth Turshen, 'Trends in the Health Sector with Special Reference to Africa,' unpublished paper, Rutgers University, New Brunswick, NJ, 1993.
19. Jespersen, p. 40.
20. United Nations, *Financing Africa's Recovery: Report and Recommendation of the Advisory Group on Financial Flows for Africa* (New York: United Nations, 1988), p. 17.
21. Schoepf et. al., cited in Meredeth Turshen, 'Trends in the Health Sector with Special Reference to Africa', unpublished paper, Rutgers University, New Brunswick, NJ, 1993, p. 12.
22. Lawrence Altman, '"Catastrophe" of Cholera is Sweeping Africa,' *New York Times*, July 23, 1991, pp. B7, B8.
23. Wright and McManus, p. 207.
24. UNDP, p. 36.
25. Ibid.
26. Quoted in Morris Miller, *Debt and the Environment: Converging Crises* (New York: United Nations, 1991), p. 70.
27. World Bank, *The Third Report on Adjustment Lending: Private and Public Resources for Growth* (World Bank: Washington, DC, 1992), p. 19.
28. Ibid., pp. 19–20.
29. Interview with Southeast Asian expert on rural poverty who wishes to remain anonymous, Bangkok, June 24, 1993.
30. United Nations Children's Fund (UNICEF), *The State of the World's Children* (New York: Oxford University Press, 1993), p. 69.
31. World Bank, *World Development Report 1992: Development and the Environment* (Washington, DC: World Bank, 1992), p. 30.

32. Ibid., pp. 7–8.
33. Susan George, *The Debt Boomerang: How Third World Debt Harms Us All* (London: Pluto Press and Boulder, Colo.: Westview Press, 1992), p. 11.
34. Sandra Postel and John Ryan, 'Reforming Forestry,' in *State of the World* (New York: Norton, 1991), p. 77.
35. Ibid., p. 81.
36. David Hojman, *Chile: the Political Economy of Development and Democracy* (Pittsburgh, Penn.: University of Pittsburgh Press, 1993), p. 168.
37. Ibid., p. 198; Hobart Spalding, 'Devastation in the Southern Cone: the Inheritance of the Neo-Liberal Years,' *Latin American Issues*, No. 11 (1992), p. 47.
38. 'Waste Contaminates Marine Products,' *El Mercurio*, May 2, 1991; reproduced in *JPRS (Joint Publications Research Service): Environmental Issues*, July 5, 1991, p. 46.
39. John Young, 'Mining the Earth,' in *State of the World 1992* (New York: Norton, 1992), p. 110.
40. Quoted in Spalding, p. 49.
41. Alicia Korten, 'Structural Adjustment, the Environment, and the Poor: the Case Study of Costa Rica,' unpublished manuscript, Institute for Food and Development Policy, San Francisco, 1992, p. 60.
42. Ibid., p. 55.
43. 'Govt. Sues Standard Banana Company over Coastal Contamination,' *Notimex* (Mexico City), February 18, 1992; reproduced in *JPRS Environmental Issues*, April 6, 1992, p. 52.
44. Korten, pp. 54–6.
45. Jean Carriere, 'The Crisis in Costa Rica: an Ecological Perspective,' in David Goodman and Michael Redclift, *Environment and Development in Latin America* (Manchester: Manchester University Press, 1991), p. 188.
46. Alan Durning and Holly Brough, 'Reforming the Livestock Economy,' in *State of the World 1992* (New York: Norton, 1992), p. 74.
47. Ibid.
48. Ibid.
49. Development GAP, *The Other Side of Adjustment: the Real Impact of World Bank and IMF Structural Adjustment Programs* (Washington, DC: Development GAP, 1993), p. 25.
50. Hillary French, 'Reconciling Trade and the Environment,' in *State of the World 1993* (New York: Norton, 1993), p. 161.
51. Fantu Cheru, 'Structural Adjustment, Primary Resource Trade, and Sustainable Development in Sub-Saharan Africa,' *World Development*, Vol. 20, No. 4 (1992), p. 507.
52. Development GAP, p. 25.
53. Charles Abugre, 'Behind the Crowded Shelves: an Assessment of Ghana's Structural Adjustment Experience,' unpublished manuscript, Institute for Food and Development Policy, San Francisco, 1993, p. 87.
54. Wilfredo Cruz and Robert Repetto, *The Environmental Effects of Stabilization and Structural Adjustment* (Washington, DC: World Resources Institute, 1992), p. 48.

55. Freedom from Debt Coalition, *Debt and Environment in the Philippines* (Manila: Freedom from Debt Coalition, 1991), p. 14.
56. Cruz and Repetto, p. 19.
57. Ibid., p. 24.
58. Robin Broad and John Cavanagh, *Plundering Paradise* (Berkeley, Calif.: University of California Press, 1993), pp. 37–8.
59. Asian Development Bank, *Economic Policies for Sustainable Development* (Manila: Asian Development Bank, 1990), p. 49.
60. Broad and Cavanagh, p. 77.
61. Ibid., p. 78.

Chapter 7: Adjustment: the Outcome

1. Karin Lissakers, *Banks, Borrowers, and the Establishment: a Revisionist Account of the Debt Crisis* (New York: Basic Books, 1991), p. 234.
2. Ibid.; see also Susan George, 'Effects of the Debt Crisis Worsen in the Third World,' *Third World Network Features*, (Penang 1992).
3. World Bank, *World Debt Tables, 1991–92*, Vol. 1 (Washington, DC: World Bank, 1991), p. 122.
4. Morris Miller, *Debt and the Environment: Convergent Crises* (New York: United Nations, 1991), p. 64.
5. 'Solutions Pass Test of Time,' *Financial Times*, April 10, 1991.
6. United Nations, *World Economic Survey 1992* (New York: United Nations, 1992), p. 81.
7. Eva Jespersen, 'External Shocks, Adjustment Policies, and Economic and Social Performance,' in Giovanni Andrea Cornia et al., eds, *Africa's Recovery in the 1990s: from Stagnation and Adjustment to Human Development* (New York: St Martin's Press, 1992), p. 49.
8. 'Last Rites in Sight for Debt Crisis,' *Financial Times,* April 10, 1991.
9. Lester Thurow, *Head to Head: the Coming Struggle among Japan, Europe, and the United States* (New York: William Morrow, 1992), p. 215.
10. South Commission, *The Challenge to the South* (New York: Oxford University Press, 1990), pp. 72–3.

Chapter 8: Resubordinating the NICs

1. Quoted in Foreign Policy Association, 'Third World Development: Old Problems, New Strategies,' *Great Decisions '86.*
2. For an analysis of command capitalism, see Walden Bello and Stephanie Rosenfeld, *Dragons in Distress: Asia's Miracle Economies in Crisis* (London: Penguin Books, 1991), pp. 47–61.
3. Tony Michell, 'From LDC to NIC: the Republic of Korea: Employment, Industrialization, and Trade, 1961–62,' unpublished manuscript, Seoul, 1988, p. 63.
4. Shim Sung-Won, 'Pohang Iron and Steel Company: Vicissitudes: the Day of the Steel Giant,' *Business Korea*, April 1988, p. 49.
5. Henrik Hansen, 'US–Korean Relations: Trends and Outlook for 1993,' *Business Korea*, January 1993, p. 24.

6. Paul Levine, 'Korean Offshore Assembly Operations Threatened,' *Business Korea*, November 1990, p. 36.
7. 'Semiconductor Exports are Threatened,' *Business Korea*, May 1992, p. 17.
8. David Mulford, 'Remarks before the Asia-Pacific Capital Markets Conference,' San Francisco, November 17, 1987.
9. Marcus Noland, 'United States Trade Policy and the Asian Economies,' in Fu-Chen Lo and Narongchai Akrasanee, eds, *The Emerging Role of the Asian NIEs and ASEAN* (Kuala Lumpur: Asian and Pacific Development Center, 1992), p. 86.
10. Interview with Y.C. Park, senior manager, Tae Heung Ltd., by Walden Bello, Seoul, May 23, 1988.
11. Office of the US Trade Representative, '1992 National Trade Estimates Report on Foreign Trade Barriers in Korea,' Washington, DC, 1992.
12. US Dept. of Commerce, 'Korea: Background–Key Issues,' Washington, DC, November 1992.
13. Office of the US Trade Representative, '1992 National Estimates Report ...'
14. Ibid.
15. Noland, p. 85.
16. US Department of Commerce, 'Korea Background–Key Issues', Washington, DC, November 1992.
17. Quoted in Paul Levine, 'Anti-Consumption Campaign: US Questions Korean Credibility on Market Opening,' *Business Korea*, December 1990, p. 16.
18. Un-Chul Paek, 'Korea under the New World Order: Challenges and Opportunities,' *Korea's Economy 1992*, pp. 38–9.
19. 'Open Agricultural Policy: a Controversial Issue in Korea,' *Grassroots* (Seoul), 1 (Spring 1988), p. 6.
20. 'Bilateral Positions: an Exchange of Views,' *Business Korea*, April 1988, pp. 44–6.
21. Cho Soon, 'The Korean Economy at a Crossroads: a Blueprint for Internationalization,' *FYI (For Your Information)*, January 27, 1989; Kim Sam-O, 'Agriculture: Buying the Farm,' *Business Korea*, November 1989, p. 18; 'Interview with the Korean Embassy's Chang Ki-Ho: Prospects for US–Korean Trade Relations in 1992,' *Business Korea*, March 1992, p. 17.
22. Kim Sam-O, p. 18.
23. Ibid.
24. Robert Goldstein, *US Agricultural Trade Opportunities with Pacific Rim Nations,* 88–755 ENR (Washington, DC: Congressional Research Service, 1989), pp. 36–8.
25. Hwang Ui-Pong, 'The Exploding Farmers Movement and the Creation of Chonnongnyon,' *Sindong-A*, April 1989, reproduced in *Foreign Broadcast Information Service: East Asia*, August 7, 1989, p. 34.
26. Henrik Hansen, 'A New Agreement,' *Business Korea*, November 1992, p. 20.
27. US Dept. of Commerce, 'Korea: Background on Key Issues ...'
28. Mark Clifford, 'Cheap Foreign Beefs,' *Far Eastern Economic Review*, July 21, 1988, p. 58.

29. Sue Chang, 'World Shouldn't Have to Wait for an Open Market,' *Business Korea*, December 1991, p. 21.
30. Ibid.
31. Ibid.
32. 'Dear Mr. Bush,' *Business Korea*, December 1991, p. 22.
33. Ibid.
34. Noland, p. 85.
35. US Dept. of Commerce, 'Thailand,' November 1992, p. 241.
36. UNCTAD, *Trade and Development Report 1990* (New York: United Nations, 1990), p. 88.
37. Anne Krueger, 'Free Trade is the Best Policy,' in Robert Lawrence and Charles Schulze, eds, *An American Trade Strategy: Options for the 1990s* (Washington, DC: Brookings Institution, 1990), p. 76.
38. Sue Chang, 'Cracking down on Pirates,' *Business Korea*, May 1993, p. 26.
39. UNCTAD, *Trade and Development Report 1990*, p. 89.
40. Jose Antonio Ocampo, 'Developing Countries and the GATT Uruguay Round: a (Preliminary) Balance,' in UNCTAD, *International Monetary and Financial Issues for the 1990s* (New York: United Nations, 1992), p. 44.
41. Ibid., p. 44.
42. UNCTAD, *Trade and Development Report 1991* (New York: United Nations, 1991), p. 191.
43. Ibid.
44. Ocampo, p. 46.
45. Bill Rosenberg, 'Can Aotearoa Survive? Sovereignty, Transnationals, and Economic Policy,' paper presented to the Peace, Power, and Politics Conference, Wellington, New Zealand, June 4–7, 1993, p. 6.
46. Ibid.
47. Ocampo, p. 47.
48. Rosenberg, p. 6.
49. Martin Khor, 'Reassess Uruguay Round, Say International NGOs,' *Third World Network Features* (Penang, 1993).
50. Ocampo, p. 41.
51. Ibid., pp. 41–2.
52. See Chakravarthi Raghavan, *Recolonialization: GATT, the Uruguay Round, and the Third World* (Penang: Third World Network, 1990).

Chapter 9: Adjusting America

1. Ray Marshall, 'Labor in the Global Economy,' in Steve Hacker and Margaret Hallock, eds, *Labor in a Global Economy* (Eugene, Oregon: University of Oregon Labor Education and Research Center, 1991), pp. 12–13.
2. Ibid.
3. Berch Beberoglu, cited in Bennett Harrison and Barry Bluestone, *The Great U-Turn* (New York: Basic Books, 1988), p. 27.
4. Joseph Grunwald and Kenneth Flamm, *The Global Factory: Foreign Assembly in International Trade* (Washington, DC: Brookings Institution, 1985), p. 3.

5. Ibid., p. 6.
6. Ibid., p. 19.
7. Ibid.
8. Pat Choate, *Agents of Influence* (New York: Alfred Knopf, 1990), p. 82.
9. Harrison and Bluestone, p. 163.
10. Robert Greenstein and Scott Barancik, *Drifting Apart: New Findings on Growing Income Disparities between the Rich and the Poor, and the Middle Class* (Washington, DC: Center on Budget and Policy Priorities, 1990), p. 6.
11. Harrison and Bluestone, p. 163.
12. Priscilla Enriquez, 'An Un-American Tragedy: Hunger and Economic Policy in the Reagan–Bush Era,' *Food First Action Alert*, Summer 1992.
13. Michael Prowse, 'America's Poor are Very Different,' *Financial Times*, May 8, 1992, p. 12.
14. Ibid.
15. Harrison and Bluestone, p. 161.
16. Harrison and Bluestone, p. 92.
17. Quoted in Kevin Phillips, *Boiling Point: Democrats, Republicans, and the Decline of Middle-Class Prosperity* (New York: Random House, 1993), pp. 173–4.
18. Lawrence Mishel and Jared Bernstein, *The State of Working America: 1992–93* (Washington: Economic Policy Institute, 1993), pp. 3–4.
19. Michael Prowse, 'No Easy Answers to Job Questions,' *Financial Times*, July 21, 1993, p. 11.
20. Ibid.
21. Kevin Phillips, *The Politics of Rich and Poor* (New York: Random House, 1990), p. 169.
22. Mishel and Bernstein, p. 4.
23. Lenny Siegel, 'The L.A. Uprising: a Sign of the Future,' *Global Electronics*, No. 114 (May 1992), p. 2.
24. Quoted in Priscilla Enriquez, p. 4.
25. Richard Ropers, *Persistent Poverty: the American Dream Turned Nightmare* (New York: Insight Books, 1991), pp. 174–8.
26. Phillips, *The Politics of Rich and Poor*, p. 169.
27. Jeff Faux and Thea Lee, 'Implications of NAFTA for the United States: Investment, Jobs, and Productivity,' in Ricardo Grinspun and Maxwell Cameron, eds, *The Political Economy of North American Free Trade* (New York: St Martin's Press, 1993), p. 240.
28. Ibid., p. 241
29. Louis Uchitelle, 'America's Newest Industrial Belt,' *New York Times*, Section 3, March 21, 1993, p. 14.
30. Timothy Koechlin and Mehrene Larudee, cited in Faux and Lee, p. 244.
31. Uchitelle, p. 14.
32. Quoted in Phillips, *Boiling Point*, (New York: Random House, 1993), p. 175.
33. Lester Thurow, *Head to Head: the Coming Struggle among Japan, Europe, and the United States* (New York: William Morrow, 1992), p. 164.
34. Mishel and Bernstein, p. 2.

35. Ibid., p. 6.
36. Phillips, *Boiling Point,* p. 23.
37. Lawrence Mishel and David Frankel, *The State of Working America, 1990–1991* (Washington, DC: Economic Policy Institute, 1991), pp. 171, 173.
38. Ibid.
39. Michael Prowse, 'The Unhappy Politics of Race,' *Financial Times,* June 10, 1991.
40. US House of Representatives, Committee on Ways and Means, quoted in Enriquez, p. 2.
41. Physicians Task Force on Hunger in America, cited in Enriquez, p. 3; Phillips, *Boiling Point,* p. 11.
42. *Two Americas: Alternative Futures for Child Poverty in the U.S.* (Medford: Center for Hunger, Poverty, and Nutrition Policy, 1993), p. 13.
43. Stephen Rose, *Social Stratification in the United States* (New York: New Press, 1992), p. 12.
44. Priscilla Enriquez, p. 2.
45. Jeffrey Garten, *A Cold Peace: America, Japan, Germany and the Struggle for Supremacy* (New York: Times Books, 1992), p. 142.
46. Thurow, p. 157.
47. Phillips, *Boiling Point,* p. 136.
48. Victoria Griffith, 'The Intelligent Car Hits the Road,' *Financial Times,* May 21, 1993, p. 10.
49. Steven Greenhouse, 'Attention America! Snap out of It,' *New York Times,* Section 3, February 9, 1992, p. 8.
50. John Ralston Saul, *Voltaire's Bastards: the Dictatorship of Reason in the West* (New York: Free Press, 1992), p. 261.
51. John Womack, Daniel Jones, and Daniel Roos, *The Machine That Changed the World* (New York: Macmillan, 1990).
52. Koji Matsumoto, *The Rise of the Japanese Corporate System* (London: Kegan Paul International, 1991), pp. 159–60.
53. Jane Perlez, 'Toyota and Honda Create Global Production System,' *New York Times,* March 26, 1993, p. C2.
54. Quoted in ibid.
55. Garten, p. 130.
56. Ibid.
57. Ibid., p. 128.
58. Matsumoto, p. 192.
59. Thurow, ibid.
60. Matsumoto, pp. 158–9.
61. Ibid.
62. Martin Dickson and Louise Kehoe, 'The Dinosaurs Arise Again,' *Financial Times,* December 21, 1992, p. 12.
63. 'For Now', *The Economist,* July17, 1993, p. 13.
64. Louis Uchitelle, 'Strong Companies are Joining Trend to Eliminate Jobs,' *New York Times,* July 26, 1993, pp. A1, C3.

65. Barbara Kelley, 'The Down Side of Downsizing,' *Pacific News Service*, May 3–7, 1993.
66. Edward Balls, 'The U.S. Puts its Poor and Huddled Masses to Work,' *Financial Times*, January 25, 1993, p. 4.
67. 'For Now', *The Economist*, p. 13.

Chapter 10: Dark Victory
  1. Jeffrey Garten, *A Cold Peace: America, Japan, Germany and the Struggle for Supremacy* ((New York: Times Books, 1922), p. 203.
  2. Ibid.
  3. Joseph Fletcher, 'Chronic Famine and the Immorality of Food Aid: a Bow to Garrett Hardin,' *Focus*, Vol. 3, No. 2 (1993), p. 44.
  4. Ibid., p. 45.
  5. 'Blaming the Victims,' *The Economist*, June 5–11, 1993, p. 47.
  6. Jacques Attali, *Millenium: Winners and Losers in the Coming World Order* (New York: Times Books, 1991), p. 73.
  7. Ibid., p. 76.
  8. Ibid., p. 77.
  9. Ibid., p. 15.
 10. Alan Riding, 'A Surge of Racism in France Brings a Search for Answers,' *New York Times*, May 27, 1990, p. A4.
 11. Ibid.
 12. Presidential Commission on Long-Term Integrated Strategy, *Discriminate Deterrence* (Washington, DC: US Government Printing Office, 1988), p. 15.
 13. Patrick Tyler, 'Pentagon Imagines New Enemies to Fight in Post-Cold War Era,' *New York Times*, February 17, 1992, pp. A1, A5.
 14. 'Towards a Clinton Doctrine,' *The Economist*, July 17, 1993, p. 30.
 15. Barbara Crossette, 'US Aide Calls Muslim Militants Concern to the World,' *New York Times*, January 1, 1992, p. 3.
 16. Samuel Huntington, 'The Clash of Civilizations', *Foreign Affairs*, Summer, 1993, pp. 22–49.
 17. 'Living with Islam,' *The Economist*, April 4, 1992, p. 11.
 18. Jacques Attali.

Chapter 11: The Battle for the 21st Century
  1. Alain Lipietz, *Towards a New Economic Order* (New York: Oxford University Press, 1992), p. 19.
  2. See Richard Falk, *Explorations at the Edge of Time* (Philadelphia: Temple University Press, 1992).

Chapter 12: The Asian Economic Implosion
  1. Kenneth Courtis, 'Asian Crisis: More than Crony Capitalism,' *International Herald Tribune*, August 14, 1998.
  2. Ibid.
  3. *Capital Flows to Emerging Market Economies*, April 30, 1998, p. 4.

4. Jayati Ghosh and C.P. Chandrasekhar, Speech at College of Public Administration, University of the Philippines, July 3, 1998.

5. HG Asia, Communique: Thailand ('Thailand – Worth a Nibble Perhaps but not a Bite' (Hong Kong: HG Asia, 1996) (Internet version).

6. *Capital Flows to Emerging Economies*, April 30, 1998, p. 4.

7. For a good account of this episode see Eric Altbach, 'The Asian Monetary Fund Proposal: A Case Study of Regional Leadership,' *Japan Economic Institute Report*, No. 47A (December 19, 1997).

8. Larry Summers, 'American Farmers: Their Stake in Asia, Their Stake in the IMF,' Office of Public Affairs, US Treasury Dept., Washington, DC, February 23, 1998.

9. Jeffrey Sachs, 'The IMF and the Asian Flu,' *American Prospect* (March–April 1998).

10. See Joseph Stiglitz, 'More Instruments and Broader Goals: Moving towards the Post-Washington Consensus,' 1998 WIDER Annual Lecture, Helsinki, Finland, January 7, 1998.

11. Paul Krugman, 'Saving Asia: It's Time to Get Radical,' *Fortune*, September 7, 1998, pp. 33–8.

12. See, among others, Walden Bello and Stephanie Rosenfeld, *Dragons in Distress: Asia's Miracle Economies in Crisis* (London: Penguin, 1991); and Robin Broad, 'The Political Economy of Natural Resources: Case Studies of the Indonesian and Philippine Forest Sectors,' *Journal of the Developing Areas* (April 1995), pp. 317–40.

13. 'Time for Less Hectic Growth,' *Business Times*, August 20, 1997.

Appendix: Tables

Appendix 1: IMF and World Bank Stabilization and Structural Adjustment Loans, 1980–1991

Country*	SBA	EFF	SAF	ESAF	adjustment loans	Total
	In cooperation with the IMF				*In cooperation with the World Bank*	
Algeria	2				2	4
Argentina	5				6	11
Bangladesh	3	1	1	1	3	9
Barbados	1		1			2
Belize	1					1
Benin			1		2	3
Bolivia	3		1		4	8
Brazil	2	1		1	3	7
Burkina Faso			1		2	3
Burma	1					1
Burundi	1		1		3	5
Cameroon	1			1	1	3
Central African Republic	6	1			4	11
Chad			1		2	3
Chile	2	2			3	7
China	2				1	3
Colombia					4	4
Comoros			1		1	2
Congo, People's Republic of the	2				1	3
Costa Rica	6				3	9
Côte d'Ivoire	6	1			6	13
Cyprus	1	1				2
Dominica	1	1	1		1	4
Dominican Republic	2	1				3
Ecuador	4				2	6
Egypt	2				1	3
El Salvador	3				1	4
Equatorial Guinea	2		1		1	4
Ethiopia	6					6
Gabon	3	1			1	5

continued

Country*	In cooperation with the IMF				In cooperation with the World Bank	Total
	SBA	EFF	SAF	ESAF	adjustment loans	
Gambia, The	3		1		2	6
Ghana	3	1	1	1	10	16
Grenada	2			1		3
Guatemala	3					3
Guinea	3		1		3	7
Guinea-Bissau			1	1	3	5
Guyana	1	1			2	4
Haiti	3		1	1		5
Honduras	2				3	5
India	2					2
Indonesia					4	4
Jamaica	6	1			10	17
Jordan	1				1	2
Kenya	6	1	1		7	15
Korea, South	3				3	6
Lao People's Democratic Republic	1		1		1	3
Lesotho			1			1
Liberia	5			1		6
Madagascar	7	1	1		4	13
Malawi	5	1			6	12
Mali	7			1	4	12
Mauritania	5		1		5	11
Mauritius	5			1	3	9
Mexico	3	3			13	19
Mongolia	1					1
Morocco	6	2			8	16
Mozambique			1		2	3
Nepal	1		1	1	2	5
Nicaragua	2					2
Niger	4		1		2	7
Nigeria	2			1	4	7
Pakistan	8	2	1		7	18
Panama	4				2	6
Papua New Guinea	2				1	3
Paraguay						0
Peru	2	1				3
Philippines	5	2			8	15
Rwanda	1		1		1	3
São Tome and Principe			2		2	4
Senegal	6	1	1	1	5	14

continued

Appendix 1 *continued*

Country*	In cooperation with the IMF				In cooperation with the World Bank	Total
	SBA	EFF	SAF	ESAF	*adjustment loans*	
Sierra Leone	3	1	1		1	6
Solomon Is.	2					2
Somalia	5		1		2	8
South Africa	1					1
Sri Lanka	1		1	1	2	5
Sudan	2				2	4
Tanzania	2		1	1	4	8
Thailand	3				2	5
Togo	6		1	1	5	13
Trinidad and Tobago	1				1	2
Tunisia	2	1			5	8
Turkey	1				10	11
Uganda	4	1	1		4	10
Uruguay	5				4	9
Venezuela		1			5	6
Western Samoa	3					3
Zaïre	6	1	1		2	10
Zambia	3	1			5	9
Zimbabwe	2	1			1	4
Total	240	34	34	17	241	566

*Note: Eastern European countries have been excluded from this table, as most are not considered part of the Third World.

Legend: SBA = Standby Arrangement; EFF= Extended Fund Facility; SAF= Structural Adjustment Facility; ESAF= Enhanced Structural Adjustment Facility.

Sources: *IMF Annual Report, 1980–1991*; World Bank, *The Third Report on Adjustment Lending: Private and Public Resources for Growth*, Washington, 1993.

Appendix 2: Rates of Poverty and Indigence in Selected Latin American Countries

	Percentage of Households in Poverty and Indigence					
	National Average		Urban		Rural	
Countries	Poverty	Indigence	Poverty	Indigence	Poverty	Indigence
Argentina						
1970	8	1	5	1	19	1
1980	9	2	7	2	16	4
1986	13	4	12	3	17	6
Brazil						
1980	39	17	30	10	62	35
1990	43	20	39	17	56	31
Colombia						
1980	39	16	36	13	45	22
1986	38	17	35	12	42	22
Costa Rica						
1980	22	6	16	5	28	8
1990	24	10	22	7	29	12
Chile						
1970	17	6	12	3	25	11
1986	38	14	37	13	45	16
1990	35	12	34	11	36	15
Guatemala						
1980	65	33	41	13	79	44
1986	68	43	54	28	75	53
Honduras						
1970	65	45	40	15	75	57
1986	71	51	53	28	81	64
1990	75	54	65	38	84	66
Mexico						
1970	34	12	20	6	49	18
*1980	–	–	–	–	–	–
1986	30	10	23	6	43	19
*1990	–	–	–	–	–	–
Panama						
1980	36	19	31	14	45	27
1990	38	18	34	15	48	25
Peru						
1970	50	25	28	8	68	39
1980	46	21	35	12	65	37
1986	52	25	45	16	64	39
Uruguay						
1970	–	–	10	4	–	–
1980	11	3	9	2	21	7
1986	15	3	14	3	23	8
Venezuela						
1970	25	10	20	6	36	19
1980	22	7	18	5	35	15
1990	34	12	33	11	38	17

*Figures unavailable.
Source: UN Economic Commission for Latin America (ECLA), 'Latin American Poverty Profiles for the Early 1990s', Santiago, 1992.

Appendix 3: External Accounts of Selected Third World Countries, 1982 and 1991

Country	Total external debt (in millions of US dollars)		Ratio of total debt service to exports of goods and services (%)		Ratio of total external debt to GNP (%)	
	1982	1991	1982	1991	1982	1991
Algeria	17,636	28,636	31	68	40	70
Argentina	43,636	63,707	50	48	84	49
Bangladesh	5,015	13,051	20	20	39	56
Brazil	92,990	116,514	81	31	35	28
Chile	17,315	17,902	71	34	77	61
Colombia	10,306	17,369	30	35	27	44
Costa Rica	3,645	4,043	21	18	168	56
Côte d'Ivoire	7,862	18,847	46	39	111	223
Ecuador	7,705	12,469	78	32	67	115
Ghana	1,475	4,209	16	27	37	67
Indonesia	24,732	73,629	18	33	27	66
Malawi	857	1,676	34	23*	77	79
Malaysia	13,354	21,445	11	8	52	48
Mexico	86,019	101,737	57	31	53	37
Morocco	12,535	21,219	43	28	85	80
Niger	957	1,653	55	47	51	73
Nigeria	12,954	34,497	16	25	17	109
Pakistan	11,633	22,969	16	23*	38	50
Papua New Guinea	1,628	2,752	25	29	72	84
Peru	10,712	20,708	49	27	45	43
Philippines	24,551	31,897	43	23	67	70
Tanzania	2,915	6,459	29	27*	51	251
Thailand	12,238	35,828	21	13	35	39
Tunisia	3,772	8,296	16	23	48	66
Turkey	19,709	50,252	30	31	38	48

* 1990 figure (latest available)

Sources: *IMF International Financial Statistics Yearbook, 1992;* World Bank *World Debt Tables 1992–1993,* (Washington, 1993).

Appendix 4: Voluntary Export Restraints and Related Measures Imposed by the US, 1980–1991

Target country or region	Number of export restraints	Exports affected
Argentina	2	W, selective textiles
Australia	2	Steel and steel products, bovine meat
Austria	1	Steel and steel products
Bangladesh	3	C, MMF, SBOV
Brazil	6	Steel and steel products, C, W, MMF, comprehensive, machine tools
Canada	1	Steel and steel products
China	7	Steel and steel products, C, W, MMF, SBOV, comprehensive, tungsten products
Costa Rica	3	C, MMF, selective textiles
Czech and Slovak Federal Republic	1	Steel and steel products
Czechoslovakia	3	W, MMF, selective textiles
Dominican Republic	2	C, MMF
Egypt	3	C, W, MMF
El Salvador	1	C
European Community	1	Steel and steel products
Fiji	2	C, MMF
Finland	1	Steel and steel products
Germany	2	Steel and steel products, machine tools
Guatemala	1	C
Haiti	2	C, MMF
Hong Kong	4	C, W, MMF, SBOV
Hungary	4	Steel and steel products, C, W, MMF
India	4	C, W, MMF, SBOV-apparel
Indonesia	4	C, W, MMF, SBOV
Italy	1	Machine tools
Jamaica	3	C,W, MMF
Japan	7	Steel and steel products, C, W, MMF, machine tools, passenger cars, semi-conductors
Korea, South	16	Steel and steel products, C, W, MMF, SBOV, machine tools, VCRs, TV sets, microwave ovens, footwear, stuffed toys, pianos, leather bags, fishing rods, tarpaulin products and brassware
Macau	4	C, W, MMF, SBOV
Malaysia	4	C, W, MMF, SBOV

continued

Appendix 4 *continued*

Target country or region	Number of export restraints	Exports affected
Mauritius	4	C, W, MMF, SBOV
Mexico	4	Steel and steel products C, W, MMF
Nepal	1	C
New Zealand	1	Bovine meat
Nigeria	1	C
Pakistan	3	C, MMF, SBOV-apparel
Peru	3	C, W, MMF
Philippines	3	C, W, MMF
Poland	4	Steel and steel products, C, W, MMF
Romania	1	Steel and steel products
Russian Federation	1	C
Singapore	4	C, W, MMF, machine tools
Spain	1	Machine tools
Sri Lanka	4	C, W, MMF, SBOV
Sweden	1	Machine tools
Switzerland	1	Machine tools
Taiwan	6	C, W, MMF, SBOV, machine tools, textiles and apparel
Trinidad and Tobago	4	Steel and steel products, C, MMF, selective textiles
Turkey	2	C, MMF
United Arab Emirates	4	C, MMF, SBOV, selective textiles
United Kingdom	1	Machine tools
Uruguay	2	C, W
Venezuela	1	Steel and steel products
Yugoslavia	4	Steel and steel products, C, W, MMF
Third World Countries	125	
Developed Countries	31	

Legend: C = cotton; MMF = manmade fabric; SBOV = W = wool.
Source: *GATT Trade Policy Review (United States) vol. 1, GATT Publication Services, Geneva, April, 1992.*

Appendix 5: Shares of US Family Income Going to Various Fifths, and to Top 5%, 1973–1991

Year	Lowest Fifth	Second Fifth	Middle Fifth	Fourth Fifth	Top Fifth	Total	Breakdown of Top Fifth	
							Top 5%	Next 15%
1973	5.5	11.9	17.5	24.0	41.1	100%	15.5	25.6
1979	5.2	11.6	17.5	24.1	41.7	100%	15.8	25.9
1989	4.6	10.6	16.5	23.7	44.6	100%	17.9	26.7
1991	4.5	10.7	16.6	24.1	44.2	100%	17.1	27

Source: Economic Policy Institute, Washington, D.C.

Appendix 6: Changes in Distribution of US Net Worth, 1962–1989

Wealth Class	Percent of Net Worth		
	1962	1983	1989
Top Fifth	81.7	81.5	84.3
Richest 0.5%	25.2	26.2	30.3
Next 0.5%	8.2	7.8	8.0
Next 4%	21.6	22.1	21.6
Next 5%	12.4	12.1	11.3
Next 10%	14.3	13.3	13.1
Four-Fifths	18.3	18.5	15.7
Fourth	12.9	12.5	13.0
Middle	5.2	5.2	2.7
Second	0.8	1.1	0.2
Lowest	-0.5	-0.3	-0.2
Total	100	100	100

Source: Economic Policy Institute, Washington, D.C.

Glossary

Anti-dumping order   A unilateral order imposed by the United States in which the US government reserves the right to apply sanctions against trading partners believed to be selling their goods below a reasonable rate of return in the United States. US trading partners most heavily affected by anti-dumping investigations and orders during the period July 1989 to June 1991 were China, Japan, Germany, the UK, and Taiwan. During this period, punitive duties were imposed most frequently on imports from China, Japan, South Korea, and Taiwan.

Baker Plan   Plan proposed by the then US secretary of the Treasury, James Baker, in 1985, in response to the Third World debt crisis. The main thrust of the plan was the infusion of US$20 billion in commercial bank loans and $9 billion in multilateral bank credits into 15 highly indebted countries, in return for the latter's commitment to initiate market-oriented reforms or structural adjustment.

Billion   1,000,000,000.

Containment liberalism   US Cold War strategy, which was a combination of anti-communist foreign policy and liberal domestic policy.

Deregulation   A term that refers to a policy of dismantling government controls on business activities enforced by regulatory commissions. Historically, regulation has sought both to contain the power of monopolies and to prevent destructive competition where it threatens to occur.

Downsizing   A euphemism for slashing the workforce, wages, and/or facilities, to achieve greater profitability.

Export-orientation   A policy prescribed for Third World countries by the World Bank and the International Monetary Fund that emphasizes production for exports, through low-wage labor, of manufactures like textiles and household appliances for advanced industrial countries.

GATT (General Agreement on Tariffs and Trade)   A multilateral agency that provides the framework for negotiations on international trade in commodities, agriculture, manufactures, and services. GATT negotiations have generally aimed at liberalizing international trade in goods and services through tariff cuts and the dismantling or lowering of non-tariff barriers.

Group of 77   Quasi-official group of Third World countries that loosely coordinate their stands in negotiations with advanced industrialized countries. Originally made up of 77 members, this group now encompasses well over 100 countries.

GSP (General System of Preferences)   A program in which developed countries grant trade preferences to Third World countries with the rationale of assisting their development. The GSP of the United States covers a limited number of products and, as of 1985, denies future benefits to countries with per capita incomes over US$8,500. The U.S. has increasingly conditioned the granting of preferences to the opening of the beneficiaries' markets on US exports.

IDA (International Development Agency)   This World Bank affiliate was established in 1960 in response to the demands of developing countries for increased loans on more flexible terms than those originally offered by the World Bank.

MFA (Multifiber Agreement)   A multilateral agreement entailing export restraints and regulations on the trade of textiles and clothing. In 1990, about 90 per cent of textile imports and about 85 per cent of clothing imports into the United States came from MFA members.

NAFTA (North American Free Trade Agreement)   A proposed free trade agreement among the United States, Mexico, and Canada. NAFTA would lower barriers to goods exported and imported between these countries and remove most barriers that deter corporations in one country from investing in another.

New or neo-New Deal state   A regime to regulate the capitalist economy through a combination of massive defense spending to contain international communism and enough social spending to keep domestic peace. Named after Franklin Delano Roosevelt's New Deal, which set the agenda and ideology of modern liberalism, the neo-New Deal state combines government manipulation of macroeconomic trends via fiscal and monetary mechanisms to achieve stable growth.

NICs (newly industrializing countries)   Third World countries that have realized very rapid growth in their manufacturing sectors and have developed export industries capable of competing in overseas markets. These countries include Singapore, South Korea, Taiwan, and the British crown colony of Hong Kong. In the 1960s and 1970s the NICs were praised by the US as free-market models. In the 1980s, protectionist sentiments in the North surfaced and various goods produced by the NICs came up against import barriers from the US and other global powers.

NIEO (new international economic order)   A South-backed international economic system in opposition to the current North-dominated order. The historical roots of the NIEO can be traced to the 1970s, when developing countries began forming a united front for dealing with advanced capitalist countries. Viewed as an alternative to the current exploitative system, the NIEO demands a deconcentration of wealth and promotion of equality among states through a North-to-South transference of global economic benefits.

PL-480   US system of subsidized agricultural exports to Third World countries, ostensibly created to aid in their development but which actually led to the bankruptcy of Third World farmers.

Reaganism   Ideology of the US Republican administrations of 1981–92, which espoused rollback of government and labor from the domestic economy and of the South or Third World in the international economy. Reaganism believed in deregulating both the international and domestic economies to release the 'magic of the market.'

Service Industry   The non-manufacturing sector of a country's economy, ranging from security services and office-cleaning to data-processing and teaching. A large part of what are now called 'services' are no more than packaged traditional activities connected with industry and commerce. Many of these activities involve no foreign direct investment and little transfer of technical know-how.

Special 301 Clause   A provision of the US Trade Act of 1988 in which the United States places countries on watch lists for possible trade retaliation for intellectual property rights violations.

Structural Adjustment   A euphemism used for a program of wrenching change in a Third World economy in return for loans from commercial banks, the World Bank, and the International Monetary Fund. Among the elements of structural adjustment are privatization of government enterprises, drastic reduction of the government budget deficit, devaluation of the currency, elimination of subsidies, elimination of price controls, dismantling of trade and investment barriers, and cuts or restraints on wages. The objective of structural adjustment programs is to shift much of production from the domestic market to export markets. Thus, structural adjustment programs have been attacked as thinly veiled attempts to raise foreign exchange earnings in order to pay off a country's debt.

Super 301   A clause of the US Omnibus Trade Act, which empowers the US Trade Representative to take a broad range of retaliatory measures against those countries judged to be unfair traders.

Terms of trade   The ratio of export prices to import prices. Prices for commodity exports vary erratically in the short run and fall in the long run, while the prices of manufactured imports increase steadily. Therefore, a greater amount of one's agricultural exports is needed to purchase the same amount of manufactured imports.

Trillion   1,000,000,000,000.

TRIMs (trade-related investment measures)   A set of measures proposed by Northern countries which seeks to eliminate development-related restrictions on foreign investment to allow unrestricted access of foreign capital to Third World markets.

TRIPs (trade-related intellectual property rights)   A set of measures proposed by the United States and other economic powers which strengthens patent, trademark, and royalty conventions favoring multinational corporations to restrict the diffusion of technological advances to the Third World.

UNCTAD (United Nations Conference on Trade and Development)   A UN agency established in the early 1960s that is seen by the United States and other economic powers as promoting primarily a pro-Third World economic agenda.

Uruguay Round   The eighth and current set of multilateral trade negotiations under the General Agreement on Tariffs and Trade. Launched in September 1986, the Uruguay Round has 14 items on the agenda of trade in goods. One of the two main foci is lowering tariffs on goods and reducing barriers to the free flow of agricultural products. A second focus for negotiation in the Uruguay Round is to set a global framework trade in services (such as insurance and data-processing) and intellectual property rights (such as books and computer software). The Uruguay Round is an ambitious attempt to establish a new international trade regime and institutionalize the hegemony of multilateral corporations.

USTR (United States trade representative)   US government office that functions as the US trade policy coordinator for the executive branch, Congress, and the private sector.

VERs (voluntary export restraints)   Self-imposed quotas adopted by exporting countries in fear of retaliation from the importing country. The primary sectors subject to VERs include automobiles, footwear, steel, ships, electronic products, and machine tools. Of the roughly 100 functioning VERs, 55 restrict exports to the European Community and 32 restrict exports to the United States.

Selected Readings

Bernard Nossiter's *The Global Struggle for More* (New York: Harper and Row, 1987) provides a comprehensive account of the development of the North–South competition from the 1950s to the 1980s.

The assumptions, perspectives, and policies of containment liberalism are ably analyzed by Jerry Sanders in *Peddlers of Crisis: the Committee on the Present Danger and the Politics of Containment* (London: Pluto Press, 1983). Also useful are Patrick Lloyd Hatcher's *The Suicide of an Elite: American Internationalists and Vietnam* (Stanford, CA: Stanford University Press, 1990) and Deborah Shapley's *Promise and Power: The Life and Times of Robert McNamara* (Boston: Little, Brown, 1993).

On the development of Rollback Republicanism, Franz Schurmann's *The Logic of World Power* (New York: Pantheon, 1974) is still unsurpassed for its analysis. Trenchant presentations of the right-wing view of the South are found in *U.S. Aid and the Developing World* (Washington, D.C.: Heritage Foundation, 1985) and Peter Bauer and Basil Yamey, 'Foreign Aid: What is at Stake?', *The Public Interest*, Summer 1982.

Probably the best accounts of the debt crisis yet to appear are Karin Lissakers' *Banks, Borrowers, and The Establishment: A Revisionist Account of the International Debt Crisis* (New York: Basic Books, 1991) and Susan George's *A Fate Worse Than Debt* (San Francisco: Food First, 1988).

On the dynamics and consequences of structural adjustment, among the most useful works are the following: Giovanni Andrea Cornia et al., eds., *Africa's Recovery in the 1990s: From Stagnation to Human Development* (New York: St. Martin's Press, 1992); Jose Maria Fanelli, Roberto Frenkel, and Lance Taylor, 'The World Development Report 1991: A Critical Assessment,' in *International Monetary and Financial Issues for the 1990s* (New York: United Nations Conference on Trade and Development, 1992); Mohsin Khan, 'The Macroeconomic Effects of Fund-Supported Adjustment Programs,' *International Monetary Staff Papers,* Vol. 37, No 2 (June 1990); Peter Robinson and Somsak Tambunlertchai, 'Africa and Asia: Can High Rates of Growth Be Replicated?', *Occasional Papers*; International Center for Economic Growth, No. 40 (1993); Simon Teitel, ed., *Towards a New Development Strategy for Latin America* (Washington, D.C.: Inter-American Development Bank, 1992); and Development GAP, *The Other Side of Adjustment: The Real Impact of World Bank and IMF Structural Programs* (Washington, D.C.: Development GAP, 1993).

Two good case studies of structural adjustment that will soon be published by Food First are Charles Abugre's 'Behind the Crowded Shelves: An Assessment of Ghana's Structural Adjustment Experience' (Food First, San Francisco, 1993); and Alicia Korten's 'Structural Adjustment, The Environment, and the Poor: The Case Study of Costa Rica' (Food First, San Francisco, 1992).

On the emergence of the NICs, see Walden Bello and Stephanie Rosenfeld, *Dragons in Distress: Asia's Miracle Economies in Crisis* (London: Penguin, 1991). On the use of super 301 and other bilateral weapons, see UNCTAD, *Trade and Development Report 1990–93* (New York: United Nations, 1990–93). On the consequences of GATT for the South, the best reference is undoubtedly Chakravarthi Raghavan, *Recolonization: GATT, the Uruguay Round, and the Third World* (Penang: Third World Network, 1990). See also Jose Antonio Ocampo, 'Developing Countries and the GATT Uruguay Round: A (Preliminary) Balance,' in UNCTAD, *International Monetary and Financial Issues for the 1990s* (New York: United Nations, 1992).

Among the best analyses of the dynamics of corporate capital's restructuring of the US economy are Joseph Greenwald and Kenneth Flamm's *The Global Factory: Foreign Assembly in International Trade* (Washington D.C.: Brookings Institution, 1985), and Bennett Harrison and Barry Bluestone, *The Great U-Turn* (New York: Basic Books, 1988).

On NAFTA, see two excellent collections: John Cavanagh, John Gershman *et al., Trading Freedom* (San Francisco: Food First, 1992); and Ricardo Grinspun and Maxwell Cameron, eds., *The Political Economy of North American Free Trade* (New York: St. Martin's Press, 1993).

On the social consequences of the corporate adjustment of America, see Kevin Phillips, *Boiling Point: Democrats, Republicans, and the Decline of Middle-Class Prosperity* (New York: Random House, 1993); Priscilla Enriquez, 'An Un-American Tragedy: Hunger and Economic Policy in the Reagan-Bush Era,' *Food First Action Alert*, Summer 1992; and Lawrence Mishel and Jared Bernstein, *The State of Working America: 1992–93* (Washington: Economic Policy Institute, 1993).

On insightful comparisons among the Anglo-American, Japanese, and German variants of capitalism, see Koji Matsumoto, *The Rise of the Japanese Corporate System* (London: Kegan Paul International, 1991); John Womack, Daniel Jones, and Daniel Roos, *The Machine that Changed the World* (New York: Macmillan, 1990); and Lester Thurow, *Head to Head: The Coming Struggle Among Japan, Europe, and the United States* (New York: William Morrow, 1992).

On alternative futures, see, for the bleak version, Jacques Attali, *Millennium: Winners and Losers in the Coming World Order* (New York: Times Books, 1991); and, for the optimistic one, Alain Lipietz, *Towards a New Economic Order* (New York: Oxford University Press, 1992). Richard Falk's *Explorations at the Edge of Time* (Philadelphia: Temple University Press, 1992) is an exciting effort to chart the shape and direction of Post-Cold War social movements.

Index

157